HOW TO
BECOME
FEARLESS

*A Practical Guide for Destroying Fear
and Living with Freedom*

Jay Mistry

First Edition, 2020

www.jaymistry.net

ISBN: 979-8-67-334683-9

CONTENTS

HOW TO

BECOME

FEARLESS

INTRODUCTION

WHY THIS BOOK WAS WRITTEN

"Ok. Fuck it! I'll do it!"

It was close to 10 minutes earlier since I had spotted the pretty girl in the gym. She was in conversation with two jacked guys. Even though I was on the other side of the gym, I could see the veins in their chest bulging out of their XXL sized vests. And sure, they probably couldn't scratch their own backs without exerting some serious force or bringing in a third party, but they had the confidence I didn't have. They owned their space. It wasn't just their physical stature that was impressive, but their demeanour and mindset communicated a lively spirit that was attractive.

While the three of them were chatting and laughing together, which pushed me deeper into my mind, more fear washed over me. Now, if I wanted to make any impact at all, I felt like I had to top their interaction, be funnier, be cooler, and have more chemistry than the threesome did.

But I knew I just didn't know how to make the interaction last, or be leading, or be intentional, to make something beautiful happen. I didn't even know the first thing I would say.

Rewind a few minutes earlier and you'll hear me saying a number of reasons why I couldn't approach the pretty girl at the gym. I was with a guy who didn't give a fuck about social niceties. He would do shit just because he knew it could be done. Also, because he just wanted to. He didn't overthink things, he just genuinely acted instead. He found out for himself. He trusted his abilities and had enough personal reference experiences of taking action so that this wasn't a big issue for him.

So, whilst we were talking, and I shared my interest of the pretty gym goer, he said something to the effect of, "Bro, don't be a bitch, just go over there".

The reasons just kept on coming. "She's talking with others. It's rude to just speak to someone out of the blue. It's weird. What do I say?"

The two hulks left her to it, and she went back to pushing the weights on the leg press. She finished her set. "It's now or never", I said to myself, still full of nerves and clueless as to how this was going to go.

Realising I was being a little bitch, I just said, "Ok. Fuck it! I'll do it!"

As I walk over my legs began to shake, even though today was an upper body work out day. My hands got hot and clammy. My voice softened and retracted in me, just like other parts of my anatomy, and all I wanted to do was crawl up into a ball and let this be over with as soon as possible.

I get around 5 metres away from her and I can't believe

I'm even attempting to do this. It's happening! My heart rate increases and furiously pumps away. Mentally, I'm too preoccupied to think anything other than getting over to her. After another couple of steps in, she notices me in her work out space. One more step and I'm at an appropriate distance from the pretty girl. I look at her, she looks at me, I force a smile, she looks at me with a neutral face. I realise it is up to me to make her smile or have her tell me, "Fuck off, you loser!"

I open my mouth, and for a split second I think about asking her, "How many sets do you have left?". If I do that, the whole build up and prior 10 creepy minutes of admiration would have been a waste. I would have felt like shit, knowing I gave in to my emotions and bitched out at the very last second. I couldn't let myself live with it and didn't want to remember this as a failure of not even trying. To add to it, I would have to come up with a soppy explanation to tell my friend of why I didn't go for it. That would have been a sad attempt to justify a weak mind state that would have been the real issue that overpowered me.

So, I switched that voice off and went in for the kill. "Hi", I said whilst panting, despite not exerting any effort for the last few minutes. It was the breathlessness that came from being in shock and needing to flood my body with oxygen before I passed out from panic. I continued, "I think you look really nice, where are you from?". She responded, "Brazil", with the slightest smile and a reluctant side-glance designed to mask the level of pity she felt for me. I replied, "That's cool. Well, nice to meet you."

I left her to get back to her workout. She could have been more responsive had I just stayed in the conversation and learned more about her. But to me, the job was done! I overcame my fear of approaching her and standing in the face of rejection. I came out unscathed, and I was over the moon.

I returned to my friend. He asked, "So, what happened?". I replied with a big smile on my face, "I asked her where she was from and she said Brazil."

"What… is that it?", my friend replied, expecting much more.

"Yep, that's it", I exclaimed, with joy beaming from my entire soul.

We both burst out laughing at my timid attempt to woo her. My friend, whilst in between fits of laughter, gave me pointers of what I should have said and done to have made it last longer and gone better, but I left that day knowing I was capable of much more than I had ever considered.

It doesn't sound much to most people who are more comfortable with the prospect of speaking with strangers, let alone pretty members of the opposite sex who excite all the senses, but for me this was a win of exceptional importance and grandeur. If I could overcome this, anything else could be done too! And so, I began a life of deliberately facing fears to bring more amazing experiences into my life.

Prior to this point, for years if not decades, I would pass situations and not even attempt to tackle the mental obstruction. I would go around it, living a life of quiet desperation. Wanting more, but pathetically settling for less than satisfactory results. I would convince myself I didn't want it anyway. I would twist it in my mind, so I felt clever and superior for sidestepping around the situations that fear stopped me from facing. But deep down I knew I was not living up to where I could have been, and even deeper down, I knew I was not happy about doing this to myself.

WHO THIS BOOK WAS WRITTEN FOR

"The mass of men lead lives of quiet desperation."
- Henry David Thoreau

'Desperation' or 'despair' is a mental state which millions of people live in on a day-to-day basis. It doesn't care if you are in a developing country or if you are in the nation with the highest average income worldwide. Money cannot change it. Only being fulfilled can change it. Freedom is true, raw, and unfiltered expression.

In simpler terms, this means someone can do something without fears of being judged or criticised. It means someone can act in a way that is true to themselves. It is living in such a way that allows for no residual emotional or physical build up. It is living in the moment. It is living being free. It is living in a way where nothing is held back, allowing a person to fully express who they are and not be attached to the outcome.

But this is something that is not taught in school. This is something most people gloss over, even though their whole sense of satisfaction is based on it. For most people it isn't in their realm of awareness, so they don't know they should learn about it. It is suppressed common knowledge. It is available to everyone with a pulse and a working brain. However, it is the most powerful resource that has not been tapped into because of its ambiguity, because it is not a physical entity to be cut open and analysed. The mind and body always seek the path of least resistance. However, this entity is only mastered through experience and by wading through the mind and body's natural tendency to avoid and let pass. This entity is fear.

Fear is the factor that holds you back from anything. Whether it is fear of public speaking, fear of rejection, fear of being different, fear of asking for the sale, fear of finding the one, fear of being alone, the fear of dying, and countless other fears.

Your brain is wired to send alert signals to your body, making you feel discomfort and anxiety when a fearful situation comes up. Floods of disastrous images crash your mind, blocking your ability to reason and process information logically. It paralyses you into not attempting to do things or stopping completely. It is the gateway for procrastination, as you put off the things you know you need to do but are daunted by. It limits your potential. It comes with its own backing soundtrack in the form of the voice of your mind, which is quick to side with the fear and convinces you that you don't need to take on the task at hand. It is cunning, it is sly, and it will steal the life right from under your nose as you try to keep safe and careful, tip-toeing around in life, never truly and fully putting yourself out into any endeavour. It can convince you to put one foot in, but more importantly have one foot out, with most of your weight on your back foot, ready to retract at a moment's notice when things seem too uncertain and up in the air.

This can happen for a lifetime. Millions of people have died never committing to giving their fullest, to trying new things, to love fully, to experience life, just in case something 'bad' 'might' happen. Then eventually for everyone their last day comes, and a lifetime of regrets can't be suppressed any longer. The bubbles rise to the surface and face the individual, shining a light on all the opportunities they wasted in their life. The one life they get, down the drain, all done, timed out!

It's the bitterest of pills to swallow, and nothing can take the taste away of that last pill. Only they would know the extent to which they pussied out. They would have no more energy to give to the world, and they would have to die knowing and regretting what their life could have been had they been fearless and acted in line with their gut instincts and intuitions.

Fear can be crippling. It can paralyse you. It can make you do stupid things, things you wouldn't normally do if you were in the right state of mind. It clouds your judgement. It makes you hesitant. It makes you think and focus on the worst-case scenario and blows up the situation to such an exaggerated and likely impossible scene.

But it is not real. Wait... What's that now?! Yes, fear... is not real! It has the ability to grossly exaggerate the truth and what is real. Fear can send us into a downward spiral which is a gateway for other negative emotions such as: disappointment, doubt, worry, blame, discouragement, anger, revenge, hatred, rage, jealousy, insecurity, guilt, unworthiness, grief, depression, powerlessness, and victimisation.

People who experience these emotions can suffer from days, weeks, years or even a lifetime of negative thinking. But there is hope. How? By harnessing fear. Fear will never go away. We are hard-wired to have it with us for life. Sorry to be the bearer of bad news. But before you go and use this book as a door stop, read on, and you'll grasp: why we fear, what fear does to us, how it changes our state, what you can do to get out of that state, and how to move into action by using and harnessing fear, instead of having fear use and abuse you!

AIM OF THIS BOOK AND EXPECTED OUTCOME

This book has 3 main sections to it:

1. Heightening Your Awareness of Fear
2. Reframing Fear
3. Death: The Final Element

With each section you will gain a deeper understanding of fear, what it does to us, why we feel it, and how by understanding its nature, you can use it to your advantage. It will be like having a superpower you can switch on and off whenever you like to help you advance in life.

Like many of you who decided to read this book, I have been at the mercy of my fears for the majority portion of my life. I've experienced firsthand what a destructive and energy zapping feeling fear is. There is no doubt in my mind that if I have been able to overcome my fears, then using the same path of self-discovery, you could do the same thing too.

There comes a point in your life where you get sick and tired of feeling the same way about certain things. In one area of your life you may be head-honcho, where people follow you as your certainty is comforting. Then in another area of your life, you are out of your circle of influence, you are in the big wide world and all of your leadership, influence, and demeanour goes right out of the window, leaving you at the whim of the rest of the world. And the world has no interest in slowing down for you. Instead, it does what it always does and advances at an ever-increasing rate.

It's in these moments where fear is at its greatest as the uncertainty of the world constantly bombards you. This is where, for most people, fear would win. As more and more situations arise, the average person would bend their will to be more lenient and compromising for others. Take Suzi. Suzi would step aside for a promotion because she has only been at the company for 3 months, much less time than her colleagues. Suzi would not speak up in the board room due to fears of being thought of as stupid or thinking her ideas are not up to par and good enough. Suzi convinces herself not to invite her manager out for dinner with her, even though their kids go to the same school, they have similar humour and would be best friends in another environment. But because of her fear of one of her colleagues named Linda, she doesn't. She fears Linda would start talking to others around the office about it, making fun of her and making comments here and there to single her out. All the while, Linda spends her time spreading rumours about others trying for that promotion. Linda doesn't do the work she has been assigned during the day. Instead, she steals other people's ideas and presents them as her own. Linda has a team of people who she has under her thumb by means of exclusion if they ever step out of place by questioning her authority.

We all know a 'Linda' in our lives. They make you want to rip your hair out as they play their conniving games. Well, you know what... Fuck Linda! Fuck her and her pack of pleasing, pathetic, spineless see you next Tuesdays. It's high time Suzi shook up that office place and took the initiative to make positive changes for herself, for her department, and for the good of the company. Instead of settling and being pushed aside to be just another cog in the corporate machinery, Suzi could take control and implement new initiatives to drastically change the dynamic in the company. She could put herself in a position to get that promotion, earn the respect and praise she deserves, and develop the friendships that keep bearing fruit for years to come.

But will Suzi take her shot when the opportunity comes. Two paths lay in front of her. She could step up, or she could step aside. The determining factor is what Suzi decides to do when it's crunch time. When it's fight, flight, or freeze.

In fight mode, Suzi takes on the challenge and comes out on top, winning the promotion, the friendship, and the admiration of her colleagues.

In flight mode, Suzi moves aside and lets Linda fills the spot. Suzi then continues to get stepped on, gradually going lower down in the pecking order of the company.

In freeze mode, Suzi does nothing, looking stupid and incompetent in the process. She either gets glossed over and forgotten about or is fired for a lack of contribution towards the company.

In either fight or flight mode, Suzi is in control. She can choose to play or pass. In freeze mode, Suzi lets her emotions control her and becomes useless. For the record, whether in fight, flight, or freeze modes, all states could lead to failure or success. However, choosing fight mode evokes personal satisfaction. Knowing you chose to fight gives an added boost of energy, creativity, and passion that would lack in the flight or freeze modes.

Suzi could have failed miserably, but she would not go away thinking, 'What if?'. She would have her head and heart intact as her internal moral compass knew she gave it all she had. She would have at least felt fulfilled and pleased with her courage and resolve in the situation she was in.

• • • • •

We all have a voice inside; one is your empowering self,

and one is your limiting self. The limiting self is there to preserve you as you are at this moment. It has no intention to help you advance, just to keep you as you are now. It loves the comfort zone and wants to keep you there. Unfortunately for you, nothing exciting, interesting, or fulfilling is inside the comfort zone. You have things there that keep you content and you can end up living your entire life in a comfort zone. It is a safe place, but as it is safe, not much happens there.

I knew a successful man who put it this way: "My grandmother is a beautiful woman, she took care of us growing up, raised a whole family, taught our mother how to cook, took us to school, and was always there for us, which I admire. However, she has lived in the same house for over 50 years and still to this day, she listens to the same radio she listened to when she was 50 years younger. She watches the same television she watched when she was 50 years younger. She sits in the same house she has always sat in for the last 50 years. Even the décor has stayed exactly the same, as if it was stuck in a time trap. I love my grandmother, but I don't want her life."

Through the life his grandmother lived, this man saw that the comfort place can be comfortable and pleasant, but it's not exciting. It doesn't provide the lubricant of a truly exhilarating life. No one would say, "I'm glad I didn't try new things. I like things just as they are and don't want to go anywhere or do anything out of the norm". Regret is a powerful motivator.

This book isn't for inspiring you, motivating you, or making you want to take action. Its only purpose is for you to heighten your awareness of fear. It will help you understand how fear works, it will expose different types of fear, and it will explain why you experience fear. Then, with that knowledge it will help you overcome fears in real life as you will come to know their cause, their effect, and how to control them so you are free to live your fullest life.

This book contains profanity but doesn't care about offending. This book only cares about getting you to a place where you can live truly fulfilled and happily. I hope this book provides a way for you to access your fearless state on a daily basis and allows you to take action on the path of your choosing. I'd love to hear the stories of how this book has impacted you and any experiences you had as a result of the information discussed in this book.

It is at this point I should state that all the ideas expressed in this book are not original. I have researched the work from experts in the field, read many books on the matter, and have personally applied all the principles laid out in this book. I admit to being a student of life and of great minds who have come before me. All the wisdom in this book should be credited to the experts I have been influenced by. Over the period of almost a decade, these are the lessons I have tested, with results proving reliable and working for me. This is not an exhaustive list of ideas, techniques, and principles related to fear, but I believe this book will help the lives of those who read it to become more free, uninhibited, and live fearlessly. You can use these ideas, and if they help you, that's great. If you decide to not use them, that's fine too. The ideas expressed here only work if you use them. If you agree with them, amazing, and good for you. If you disagree with any of the ideas, then that's good for you too. You should challenge thoughts and ideas to extract the best possible mindset to help you achieve more in life. What matters to me is if it works, and you can only find that out by testing the ideas out for yourself. My hope is that you use the ideas discussed in this book to live the life of your choosing and unlock the freedom available to us all by living life fearlessly.

SECTION 1:
HEIGHTENING YOUR
AWARENESS OF FEAR

Defining Fear:
noun

1. *a distressing emotion aroused by impending danger, evil, pain, etc., whether the threat is real or imagined; the feeling or condition of being afraid.*
2. *a specific instance of or propensity for such a feeling: an abnormal fear of heights.*
3. *concern or anxiety; solicitude: a fear for someone's safety.*
4. *reverential awe, especially toward God: the fear of God.*
5. *something that causes feelings of dread or apprehension; something a person is afraid of: Cancer is a common fear.*
6. *anticipation of the possibility that something unpleasant will occur: Having grown up during the Great Depression, he had a constant fear of running out of money.*

Fear is the releasing of chemicals within the body which causes various physical symptoms, such as a spiked heart rate, contracting of muscles, and restrictive breathing. Our five basic senses send information to our brains and cause an autonomic response, meaning it is involuntary and cannot be controlled. It is an entirely unconscious process that has been conditioned into humans over vast periods of time.

There are several departments inside the brain. One department raises the body's alert signals, which primes the body to do something to avoid being killed. Another department is the processing section of the brain, where information can be thought upon and rationalised to determine if the experience is life-threatening or not.

The fight-or-flight responses are summoned and stay alert until the rational department defuses the situation by deciding if the threat is over. During the fight-or-flight response, adrenaline and a cocktail of other hormones are pumped into the blood stream. Muscles tighten, the heart rate and blood pressure increase, and the body becomes very alert and ready for action.

Your pupils dilate to take in as much light as possible, your blood gets sent to major muscle groups, and your blood-glucose levels increase. The lungs take in more oxygen, while the less crucial bodily systems, like the digestive system and immune system, shut down to allow more energy for responsive actions. This is all done within seconds inside your body. It allows you to take the necessary actions to avoid being killed, and to live to see another day.

Fear is very useful. If we didn't experience fear, we would likely die very soon. It all comes down to survival. It is hard-wired into us from generations of fleeing and being killed off. For example, let's say a baby in a tribe living over 100,000 years ago walked out of its hut one day and saw a deadly snake. Like any baby, being curious and explorative is part of its nature. When seeing the snake, it's likely the baby would think, "Oh cool, a wriggly animal I can play with". As it walks over to the snake, the snake out of its own fear of being killed, or attacked, or being used as a pacifier, decides to send off a warning strike. In less time than it takes to blink your eye, the snake reacts from being in a curled 'S' shape, to darting like a bullet right towards the babies face with its fangs shown to warn off the threat. The 'threat' in this case being the bouncy, bubbly baby who wants nothing more than to have fun.

If the baby had no fear, it wouldn't think anything of the snake's initial warning pounce. He would continue to go straight for it, ending in the unfortunate demise of our cute little ancestor. He would not have reached adulthood, he would not be able to pass on his genes, and in effect, he killed off any chance of his family's bloodline living on. Only the resourceful, the instinctive, and the cream of the crop survived. Only they got the privilege of passing down their DNA to the rest of humanity. The entire human race owes their existence to those earlier humans who used fear to survive.

The rest, the ones who lacked the survival instincts, served as pillars to guide us where not to tread in case we too end up like them, extinct! We did inherit things from the extinct, but it was from their lacks, as their ways did not play out successfully and their traits led to their death. Therefore, over huge periods of time we became wired to be fearful of certain things. Now when a baby is born and gets to that curious and inquisitive age of exploration, when a snake in the wild leaps and gives him a warning shot, the baby would instinctively get shocked, perhaps flinching, becoming startled, and change its behaviour. It might cry and run back to its mother, and the experience would teach the baby not to do it again.

So, fear is a conditioning. It can be conditioned over millenniums, so it becomes wired into each living being from birth. It can also be conditioned in the short-term, happening within moments, days, weeks, years or over the course of a life. The evolutionary fears are firmly rooted and greatly benefit a person's life. However, it's the short-term conditioning, usually from our surroundings and the people closest to us, that impact the quality of our day-to-day lives.

CONDITIONED FEAR

Take Josh and Peter. Both boys are 10 years old. They both attend public schools and their families earn around the same £80,000 combined income per year. Josh's parents live in New York, USA and Peter's parents live in London, UK. Josh's dad is an accountant. Peter's dad is in marketing. Josh's mum is a lawyer. Peter's mum is a doctor.

Nothing out of the ordinary so far. Both boys live around 1 mile away from their schools. Josh's parents drive him to school. Peter's parents let him walk. Josh's parents work from home with their jobs, so they pick up Josh right after school as soon as the bell rings. He goes home, watches TV, does his homework, eats his dinner and goes to bed, ready for the same again the next day. Josh's parents prefer to pick Josh up because they are only 1 mile away from the school, it's safer for them to pick him up than letting him walk home alone, and it helps them break up their day by driving to the school and back. Peter's parents work at the office and hospital and don't finish until 6pm each night. Then, they commute to get back home around 6.30pm, so Peter spends his after school routine as follows: 4pm, finish school and head to after-school club until 6pm, then he walks home, meets his parents at 6.30pm, they eat together, enjoy family time and go to sleep, ready for the next day.

Slight differences, but over time this simple conditioning can make a big difference. At after-school club, Peter hangs out with other kids, does more socialising, has fun, and unknowingly collects positive and negative reference experiences. Peter didn't enjoy going there at first but now, after a few weeks, has built up a reputation as a fun kid. In the process he has become very confident when he's there, treating everyone like family. He even takes the newcomers under his wing. They see him as a person they enjoy being around, as he makes them feel comfortable and they enjoy being friends with him.

Josh is a good kid too, but during the time Peter is at after-school club, Josh is being picked up by his parents, driven home, followed by homework, dinner, leisure time, then bed. Nothing too exciting.

Both parents want their kids to do exceptionally well in life and both love them as much as any good parents do, but even with their best intentions, they can condition their children to fear in subtle and insidious ways. This can lead to one having better results in the long-term.

Peter goes to after-school club. There, he gets to interact with other kids, has fun, becomes more social, gets to flex his leadership skills and hone them. He gains better communication and rapport building skills, which is invaluable in the real world. He gets to learn more about himself in a group setting, which can reap bigger rewards when he's out of schooling and in jobs, relationships, and business.

Josh, despite being just as good a kid as Peter, has missed out on these hours of structured social conditioning. Peter goes to after-school club for 2 hours per day, Monday to Friday. Over the week, that's 10 hours of extra social and communication development time. That's more than another entire school day per week. Over the year, minus the 5 months off for school holidays, leaving 7 months of after-school club time available, Peter has 303 hours of extra social skill building time. That works out to around 37 extra school days per year! And when you multiply that by how many years he would attend after-school club, the result could be close to an entire year more of social development time. That could shoot Peter into becoming an elite communicator and performer later in life.

Josh gets picked up and dropped off to school. He has no time assigned for developing a skill. In the process, he's grown slightly nervous when he needs to walk to places alone. He's developed a fear of strangers and has become more on guard against people when in social settings and prefers to spend time by himself rather than with others.

This later in life, when in the working world or in business, would help Peter fly into interactions with others, giving him the upper hand when it comes to breaking the ice and creating connections. This would also help him to develop trust with others, which means more likeability, which means more sales for the company or business, which means a higher income for Peter, which results in a higher quality lifestyle.

Josh would attempt to make the same connections but would lack the depth of communication skills, making it take longer for him to build good relationships. This would mean less trust, which means fewer opportunities to seize, which means he would have a more challenging path to better his lifestyle. In romantic relationships, this could affect Josh by making it harder for him to break the ice and create a spark with someone he finds attractive. This could then lead him down a path of despair, ending with crying and drinking himself to sleep each night as he retires into his one-bed mobile home, parked in the lay-by of a motorway. Poor kid!

Okay, I'm clearly kidding with that last part! Of course, these are both grossly exaggerated stories and I'm sure that can be seen immediately, but the lesson that can be taken from this is that the conditioning from both of their parents was unintentional. Their parents would not have been aware of the long-term effects. Their intentions were good, but in this situation Josh's parents hindered his abilities, conditioning him to have weaker social skills.

The point here isn't to immediately call up your kids school and enrol them into the after-school club. That was just a silly example. The point is to bring more awareness to simple, often repeated actions that usually pass by unnoticed.

Another example could be something to the effect of Josh's parents encouraging Josh to sing in front of his extended family on Christmas day. Having received praise and admiration from his family, Josh is beaming and full of confidence. He has built a new positive reference experience to lean on for when he needs to stand in front of a room and speak, share ideas, or sing to his heart's content.

Peter used to love singing. One day when he was in the back of the car singing at the top of his lungs, his parents, who happened to be having a bad day, were getting distracted and frustrated with Peter's uninhibited singing. In anger they shouted at him, resulting in Peter feeling small, ashamed, and not worthy. Years later, when Peter is an adult, and he thinks about going for acting, singing or performing careers, he is reminded of the time his parents scolded him when he was being his most vulnerable and freest self. The situation was enough of a negative memory for Peter that before even going onto the internet to search for opportunities in the field, the fear of rejection wins, and he scraps the idea of it. He then returns to scrolling on his Facebook feed, looking at countless other people who had the courage to express themselves gaining social media stardom.

Again, clearly another example of an exaggerated story, but the principles still apply. Your evolutionary fears are good. Your conditioned fears, which started conditioning you from the day you were born, can be changed! Once you are aware of it, you can take the steps to recondition yourself. Prior to being aware of it, you will just keep bouncing around from one day to the next, never fulfilled, repeating your negative conditioning and not knowing how to get out of the rut you're in.

FEAR AND EXCITEMENT

Have you noticed when you're scared and on high alert you become more attentive, your body becomes more reactive, your muscles are ready to engage, your lungs take in more air, your hands become hot, even clammy, and your pupils dilate?

Now think about when you were excited about doing something. It may be when you were going on your first ever proper date with someone you wanted things to work out with. It could have been when you proposed to your partner, or whilst your partner was proposing to you. It could have been on your wedding day as you walk down the aisle and having everyone's eyes on you. It could have been the moments when your first child was born. It could have been in a number of situations, from getting strapped up to ride in a highly anticipated roller coaster, to the first time you had sex.

Now, choose one time you were truly excited, then close your eyes and envision it. Relive it as if you're were there now, experiencing the same moments in as much detail as you can conjure up. While you do, pay close attention to how you feel and how your body reacts.

Go on... Take a minute... I'll wait...

Now that your back here with me, it's likely you experienced some of the exact same bodily responses we described earlier that replicate the fear responses. Even as you only imagine it, and are out of the actual moment the memory was formed in, you may experience your hands getting warm, you may have taken a deep breath before going into it to allow more air to get in your lungs, your heart rate may have increased, and you may have felt as if your entire body had been activated and engaged, ready for movement.

This is because fear and excitement are the same emotion. They are the same emotion physically, but mentally they are registered in different ways. Fear makes your survival instincts kick in, whereas excitement makes your desire for pleasure take over.

Think about a surprise birthday party put together for you by your nearest and dearest. Your family set you up to have an annoying day to throw you off the scent. By the afternoon, you're pissed and frustrated that things aren't going as smooth as they should be. It's not like you ask for a lot. Just one day where things can go your way. No one has called you to wish you a happy birthday yet. It's like they have all forgotten. No happy birthday texts, flowers, or cards... nothing! What bastards!

As you walk up to your house and open the door to walk inside, hoping to get some relief from the unexciting day you just had, you're taken aback by the lights unexpectedly turning on, loud shrieks as your family shout "SURPRISE!", confetti cannons and party poppers pop off, hurtling directly towards your face, in all their colourful, stringy glory.

Your immediate reaction would not be excitement. It would be more along the lines of, "Who the fuck is in my house about to murder me?!". You'd flinch and stumble backwards as your fight, flight, or freeze modes activate. Your heart rate would immediately increase. Your eyes would dilate to take in as much light and information as possible. Your body tenses as you clutch to your belongings. Your blood pressure rises, your lungs fill with air, and a concoction of hormones flood your blood stream.

But before you run away and call the police or ball your hands into fists and start beating the living shit out of well-intentioned family members, your brains rational department overrules and decides there is no threat. In fact, this has been a well-executed plan to put the body into alert mode, and due to its highly reactive state, a great memory is more likely to be captured.

Then, as you move around the room, putting your bags down, picking drinks up, hugging your family members, and getting well wishes, your body's state is still in 'alert' mode. But this time it is 'alert' to take in as many pleasurable moments as possible. Your eyes are still dilated, your breathing is still deep, your heart rate and blood pressure are still higher than normal, and your muscles are still in action mode. But the distinction here is that you are welcoming this enjoyable experience and wishing for it to continue.

By understanding this, we can instead train and condition ourselves to be excited rather than afraid when in stressful and fear-inducing situations.

Now imagine you're walking back home from a day in the office. You take your usual way home so you're very comfortable and you know what to expect. However, as you turn into the poorly lit footpath that you must go through to get home, you notice a man's figure up ahead. You're not too worried at this point because people walk through this footpath all the time, and also because he is around the same height and build as you. But this man has his hood up, fists clenched and is walking in an antagonistic manner towards you, walking into your path rather than keeping to one side to walk past you. He's looking for trouble.

Now experience how you are feeling. Are your hands hot and clammy? Are you breathing deeper? Is your body beginning to tense? Are your eyes beginning to become super attentive? Has your heart rate elevated?

Then before you know it, he is right in front of you.

He grabs your collar and pulls you close to him, intending to intimidate you.

Now, what's your natural inclination here? If you're like most people, you would feel some panic and overwhelm as your body's fear responses kick in. But now, imagine you're excited about this situation because he's not too much bigger than you. You are confident you can win if it comes down to a fight between the two of you. You haven't been in a fight since you were at school, so you'd love to see how much damage you can cause to this ill-willed person and put them in their place. To top it off, you don't think of yourself as a wimp or someone who lets people walk all over you, so you decide to stand up for yourself.

Now the dynamic has changed. Your initially fearful state has been mentally switched to an excited state. You still have the same bodily responses, but now you are more excited than fearful about the confrontation between you and the troublemaker.

So, let's rewind. He grabs you and pulls you close to him. Then, he aggressively shouts through his teeth, "Give me everything you have on you right now or I'll beat the crap out of you!"

Now instead of retreating and giving in, your pupils still dilate, your heart rate increases, your hands flush red with the blood rushing around your body. Adrenaline is fired off left, right and centre and is courses around your veins. You react and grab hold of his throat with both hands. As you slowly and firmly squeeze your thumbs into his oesophagus, and you see the shift in his eyes from aggression to panic, to fear, to terror, a proud childlike smile beams across your face from ear-to-ear showing all your teeth as if you just won the lottery. To the mugger, it looks like you're even more of a psycho than he is.

During the choking of the unsuccessful attacker, his fear responses took over him. He went from being primed to cause harm, to not being in control, and ended with him trembling with fear as you leave him gasping for air in a puddle of his own piss.

You chose to be excited instead of scared. In a split second, you decided you wanted this moment to be registered as a win, instead of a demoralising loss. It became a life-affirming and empowering experience rather than being something you look back on as debilitating and depressing. As the event occurs and your body floods you with the alert responses, consciously registering that you are excited by the encounter empowers you to use the alert responses to your advantage.

Disclaimer: Common sense goes a long way. Silly exaggerated stories, like the above, are used throughout this book to emphasise certain points and have been written in entertaining ways only to aid in remembering the principles. The principles discussed in this book are just that, principles. The thoughts and writing in this book are in no way designed to replace a person's moral compass. For that, you'd need more than just a book to help you. The mere fact I need to write this little disclaimer is pathetic, but hey ho, it's done now, and you can go back to living your life how you see fit.

But seriously... Just be cool! Be nice, and be kind, that's all!

Just to be clear... Don't kill anyone!
Sigh

Okay. Let's continue...

UNDERSTANDING FEAR

The lack of understanding fear and how it can work for you is the main reason why people avoid it and think of it as something negative. As with anything, the more time you spend around the thing you fear, the more you understand it, and the less fearful you become of it.

As a kid growing up, I used to be frightened of cats. Not so much kittens, as they were always quite defenceless. More adult cats that had some weight to them. I couldn't see why people thought of cats as loving and adorable. I gave them as much affection as I would give a piece of toast. If I saw one out when I was walking, I would stamp my feet and pretend to lunge in its direction so it wouldn't come too close to me.

It's behaviour of fleeing when I did this, along with my uncertainty to how it would react next, further added to my fear of cats. I wasn't sure why it was doing what it was doing, and this lack of understanding, on my behalf, was enough to strike fear in me.

As time went on and I befriended new school friends, some of whom had cats, I could only play at their houses if I could get comfortable with the prospect of being around these furry felines.

A few of my classmates lived in the same area I also lived in. We would get on our bikes and ride around the area, exploring, playing and just hanging out. Jack was the kid who had all the cool things, like the keyboard, the guitar, and most importantly of all, the coveted Sony Play Station. He had the controllers, the big screen TV, all the newest games, but he also had a couple of cats.

One day a hand full of us went around to Jack's house. We took our positions on the bunk bed facing the TV, Jack put in the first multi-player game and two of my friends grabbed the controllers ready to play. I was on the lower bunk and just watching the screen. Then, out of the corner of my eye, I see a small dark creature enter the room. One of the others said welcomingly, "Oh cool, you have a cat", making it clear to me he was more comfortable with cats than I was.

A couple of them started playing with the cat, but in my mind, I was in 'flight mode'. I convincingly held it together just long enough, so the others wouldn't make a big deal out of it and shove the cat in my face. The fear I experienced felt real. My body reacted in the usual way, tensing up and being on high alert. This was clearly an uncomfortable situation for me, but I didn't have the skills or know how to handle it back then.

The cat eventually left, I casually closed the door behind it, and we carried on playing games. No one was any the wiser to my internal panic attack. Silently, I let out a sigh of relief, thankful that the 'threat' had strut away.

The fear I experienced then was the fear of the unknown. My limited experience with these creatures failed to provide me with enough positive reference experiences to reassure myself they would not harm me. I hadn't yet learned that just like every living thing, they only wanted safety, affection, and of course, tasty treats.

Hanging out at Jack's house became a regular thing for the group of us. After school, weekends, and summer holidays, when we were tired of riding our bikes, we'd end up at Jack's house, playing video games and being in the company of his cats. However, after each visit, I noticed my fear of cats gradually lessened.

Just by being around them, learning how they play with others, and seeing how they frantically ran to chase the red laser light and shoestrings, I realised that even if they were to attack me, they couldn't do much damage. I soon became comfortable with letting them sniff me so they would get comfortable with my presence. Then I moved up to scratching their heads and chins, followed by letting them sit on my lap. I soon realised my fear was totally irrational. And in fact, if I wanted to continue hanging out with my friends, then I would have to get over it.

My fear of missing out on experiences with my friends was bigger than overcoming my fear of cats. I was forced to overcome my fears to continue being in their company. To this day, people I respect, admire, and want to hang around, unknowingly push me to face many fears in my life. If I didn't do things to fit in with the crowd I want to be a part of, it would mean I would not be seen as 'one of them', which would lead to fewer invites and missing out on future plans. This process works in productive relationships, just as well as negative relationships. Having the awareness of which crowd of people will serve you best is crucial to have it work for your benefit. So, for all you kids out there, don't join gangs!

Coming back to cats. As I write this now, I have next to me, my little black and white furry beauty, Lucy, keeping me company. Her presence proves to be a great addition to the house, and she has become a loved member of the family. It seems like a massive leap from being afraid of pets, to now having one of my own. For others, it may not be cats. Many people have an over-inflated fear of spiders. But if you think about it, regarding the example of how I got over my fear, you could see how just because they have 8 legs and look almost alien compared to us, it doesn't mean at the first moment we let our guard down they will jump straight for our jugular.

In London Zoo, they host a 'friendly spider programme'. You go there and in one afternoon your fear of spiders is gone! Here's how they do it: They take you in on a crash course over a few hours. They talk about phobias. They explain spider behaviour, what they eat, how they hunt, skills they have that we don't, and explain why spiders look the way they do. You then get to meet many different kinds of spiders. In a very rational and logical way, they explain how all its bizarre features help it to survive out in the world. By the end of it you've learned so much about the spiders and have become so invested that you feel empathy for the little critters. So, when it comes time to hold them, everyone, even those who were most daunted, are ready in a single form line with their hands out and their eyes wide.

This process is excellent because it builds up positive reference experiences with the feared creature. In this case, it didn't bite you, or sting you, or leave you in a foamy spewing fit on the floor. This is good news, because now you have a story for yourself to remember and to share with others. Your perception changes. You learned more about it, and the more you understand, the less you fear. Having a calm and patient mind, with a genuine intrigue to learn more about the things you fear, is the best method to eliminate the fear completely.

If you're scared of dogs, read about them, watch videos of them playing and having fun, see how clumsy, silly, and affectionate they can be to humans who respect them. It won't take long before you start warming to them and enjoying their company.

If you're scared of flying, look into aviation. Rationalise to yourself that it is the safest form of travel, with the least number of deaths worldwide. Watch videos on how they build planes and how many safety checks are done before being allowed to leave an airport. Immerse yourself in an environment where you can learn more about the subject you fear.

If you're scared of public speaking, learn as much as you can about how to deliver an excellent, entertaining, and informative presentation. Practise in front of the mirror, then in front of your pets, then in front of your partner, then in front of the neighbourhood pets, then the real thing. Become so confident and polished in your skills you can rely on them even if you don't have any notes to read off.

"But wait a minute, what about terrorism, wars, plagues, or death?"

You're right, the things I've mentioned are fears that can be controlled. There are some fears that cannot be controlled, like a bomb blowing up a building right as you walk past it. Or a nuclear war head being dropped only 1 mile away from you, sure to obliterate everything in its path for miles. Or a disease outbreak that rapidly spreads across the planet, crippling economies and nations. These are out of your control and are popular fears held by millions of people. Later in this book is an entire section dedicated to death and things outside of your control where we will dive deeper into the matter then.

For now, think about the things you can control. Think about the irrational fears that hold you back, like public speaking, creepy crawlies, being alone, standing up for yourself in a conversation, failing, risking, being vulnerable and so on. The list is almost endless, and I'm sure you may have a specific fear in mind in relation to you. There isn't a cookie-cutter remedy for every single fear out there. This book would be too long if I tried to elaborate on all fears. However, the principles outlined in this book do apply to all fears. 'Understanding' is key in becoming free of fear. The more you understand and are around the thing you fear, the less it will take a hold of you, allowing you to become more able to deal with the situation at hand.

FEAR IN SOCIETY

We live in turbulent times where being politically correct is on high priority for a lot of people. It's a time where self-righteous opinions are on steroids. Say the wrong thing to the wrong person and sparks can start flying. Step out of your social lane and people start to question you as a person. They can turn offensive, trying to belittle your character and assassinate your reputation. The mere thought to better your life can make some people want to poke holes in your ideas and ambitions. They may laugh at you behind your back for thinking you could achieve such high goals. They may sarcastically say things like, "you've changed" or, "they've brainwashed him". This subtle and sometimes even humour-based attack is designed to keep you in your class. To keep you 'like them'. To have your head down and obediently continue with the lot you've been given so you don't disrupt their view on the world. The view they have spent decades cultivating and building walls around, that have limited them from going after their goals in life.

Your attempts to become something 'more' reveals their lost ambition, and shines a light on their levels of courage, self-worth, and self-esteem. Some may do this to keep you from the hurt of failure, as if it doesn't work out, they may be the ones to pick up the pieces, which could add to their levels of worry. Others may take the viewpoint that because you have these thoughts, you are in some way superior. They may think if you actually make a success of yourself, they will feel inferior around you. Or, it could remind them that they have decided to quit or settle in some way, and they may envy the resolve and passion you possess.

This is just one example. The truth is, there are many

other reasons that could be the cause of their attempts to limit you. It ultimately boils down to the perception of 'them' and 'us'. When you attempt to push the boundaries and explore different lifestyles, it can be taken by your original group that, in your eyes, they are now not good enough. They can feel that you are challenging their way of life, and humans by nature are creatures of habit and passionately protest change.

The fear of being judged is deep routed into our evolutionary wiring. It was a way to survive. Back in our ancestor's times, doing things too far out of the ordinary would have resulted in being ostracised. This was a real fear to be concerned with. You would not only be alone, meaning feeling unloved and discouraged, but you would also not have the benefits of living in a society where protection, food gathering, and shelter would be a collective responsibility.

The young and elderly would need more time in the confines of the village to stay safe, whereas the men would hunt and gather food. The women would take the nurturing roles based around family preservation and growth, and the fittest and strongest would be the tribe's warriors to protect the village against threats. This allowed for the village inhabitants to prosper and build bigger communities so they could live better quality lives, ensuring the survival of their kind continuing from generation to generation.

Back then it would have been more beneficial not to question or risk clashing and disrespecting members of the tribe who held more influence. It could have led to banishment and being forced to live alone, and without the tribe's contributions, your life would have been much tougher, miserable without companionship, and the risk of death would have increased considerably.

This survival instinct makes us want to adapt to societies and fit in. However, in today's world, where technology connects us with people on the other side of the planet instantaneously, and travelling from one end of the planet to the other takes less than 24 hours, being ostracised can mean you just haven't found the tribe that best suits you yet.

Let's say your family are racists but you have fallen in love with someone who is a different race than you. You know they won't mix, and they are so against it you don't even mention it to them. You fear they would disown you or even harm you over it. But you know this person is the love of your life, and you can't see any way without them because of how happy they make you feel.

Quite a pickle, right? But what would you do?

If you prefer to be happy, then falling out with your family is the consequence you would have to live with. If you prefer feeling safe within your family group, then losing a great partner is something you'd have to live with. You may decide to live a double life and hide your relationship forever, seeming single to your family, and married to the rest of the world. Although, that sounds like one slip up away from having someone's head blown off with a shotgun. Personally, I wouldn't recommend this route.

Of course, there are other options and to be honest I wouldn't like to be in this situation myself, but I do know how I would handle it. It comes down to choosing the values that are right for you.

My values are happiness and living freely and truly to myself. I enjoy doing things I enjoy, and I don't enjoy doing things I don't enjoy.

(I know, groundbreaking stuff here! But hold on...)

If the people around me don't take well to that, I can

choose to do a few things. One could be to stop associating with them and live my life with others who are more in line with my values. Another could be, if they aren't approving but will still love me anyway, I can choose to spend less time with them and live my life doing what I want away from them. Of course, each situation is different and can have more complexities, but the principle is the same. At the end of the day, it always comes down to a straightforward decision.

I understand there are oppressed people out there who are in dire situations, but ultimately a decision must be made. The solution and problem are black or white in the situation. Emotions are the grey area, but the grey area is all mind manifested. By removing the grey area and seeing it in just black or white makes it easier for you to choose which route to go down. When it comes down to it, you either execute, or you don't. You either do the thing, or you don't. You either act, or you don't. The choice is simple. You know what the answer is for you, it just comes down to execution.

Choosing to live with a free mind is a huge priority for me. To function well, my conscience needs to be clear. I need to live knowing I decided on the best choice for myself in the moment, according to my criteria for fulfilment and happiness.

I choose to not fear these emotion-filled situations because of a bigger, more empowering and higher-serving fear. That fear is to die with regret. To live knowing I wasn't my being truest self. I would be the only one to know whether my integrity was jeopardised. If it was, I would be the only one who would have to live with it. Also, it can act as a gateway for future slips of integrity, which could have a domino effect and wash away my values and moral compass entirely, leading to increasingly reckless behaviour.

This higher power fear serves me by keeping my integrity intact. It allows me to live in a way that is true to myself and overpowers any thoughts about fitting in with others. With this philosophy leading my actions, I gain more respect for myself. This healthy way of living provides me with more joy and less stress. Having your thoughts and actions aligned is freedom.

FREEZE MODE

When the mind is overloaded with sensory information, it cannot process what is happening or decide on the best thing to do. It's as if a temporary switch off and system reboot occurs. An example of this would be when something tragic happens like a bomb exploding killing people up ahead. The blast, the heat, the noise, the debris flying, and the screams of the people suffering are all a mix in the air. For most people, something like this only happens in the movies, but when it happens in real life, it can be so overwhelming that no one knows what to do. The amount of information coming at them can debilitate them leaving them 'frozen' and unable to react.

Seeing a person who was happily walking just moments ago, to now lying in front of you with their limbs decapitated from their body can be such a shock to some people that a rational response cannot be expected. Their minds processing function is paralysed and they are unable to respond appropriately. Only once the initial shock has worn off, can they return to being a functioning member of society and call the relevant authorities to get help to the crisis. During this time, people have reported to completely black out, unable to recall anything that happened whilst they were in that state of shock.

This frozen state may seem to be very impractical, but it is a trait that has been adapted and evolved over time into a useful tool to help us survive. Imagine you're walking out in the jungle, picking some berries and hunting rabbits. You wonder a little further than normal because you've found an excellent patch where lots of fresh fruit is growing. Your goal is to head back to the village to show off your magnificent jungle booty to the tribe chief's pretty daughter. You think by showing her how much of a good provider you are and how nice you treat her, she'll be swept off her feet and the two of you can spend the rest of your life watching the sun setting and getting busy creating the rest of humanity.

(**Side note**: She doesn't want the nice guy who tries hard to impress her. She wants the one she has to work for. The one who is sure of himself and is happy with or without her. The one that lives true to himself and who doesn't seek approval from anyone to do anything. But anyway, that's for another book.)

As you're finishing up in your plunder, picking the last berry your vine basket can carry, you turn around to head back to the village, but just a few metres in front of you is a colossal, hairy, 8 foot tall, 4 foot wide, 1,100 pound silver back gorilla. Oh, and let's say for the fun of it his family are with him. Some younger males, some females, and a few little ones, still hanging onto their mothers. They haven't seen you yet, but the giant is just about to turn in your direction and there's nowhere to hide. What do you do?

If you take flight and run, you will startle him, he will then slam his fists into his chest, charge right at you, grab you by the feet, spinning and smashing you into the surrounding trees, before penetrating his mandibles deep into your skull, cracking your face open, turning your brain to mush, and leaving you as a lifeless rag doll that his kids can play dress up with.

Now…

If you prime to fight mode, you charge right at him. You throw the basket and berries at him, they bounce right off his massive head, and you scream at the top of your lungs as a bluff to try to scare him off. He will then slam his fists into his chest, charge right at you, grab you by the feet, spinning and smashing you into the surrounding trees, before penetrating his mandibles deep into your skull, cracking your face open, turning your brain to mush, and you guessed it, leaving you as a lifeless rag doll that his kids can play dress up with.

Now...

What's left? Freeze mode! Ahh sweet freeze mode. Hopefully you black out so you are not present enough in your body to do something stupid, and with all the luck in the world he sees you frozen there, thinks you're no threat at all, and fingers crossed, mistakes you for something dead. Out of his own curiosity, he may come close to you and sniff around, stealing all your fruit in the process. Hopefully your paralysed state bores him enough to move on and you live to pick more fruit another day. You manage to head back to the village unscathed. Although, now you have an even bigger hole to climb out of with the tribe chief's daughter, as no matter where you are, or what era you live in, no girl is attracted to a guy who returns home with shit in his pants.

We can replace the gorilla with a wolf, or a tiger, or another large predator that could easily overpower us. In either case, we can see how the freeze mode helps us from being killed. Freeze mode benefits us when we're in such situations where playing dead is vital, however it can hinder us when we need to react and move to get out of trouble. Playing dead has its benefits when we're in the wild and walk into a bigger animal's territory. But in the world we live in today, with cities and built up communities, our lack of responding to immediate threats can harm us more than it helps us.

PAIN VS SUFFERING

"The only way to get rid of suffering is to get rid of craving. And the only way to get rid of craving is to focus on the present and to train the mind to experience reality as it is, not to daydream of how it wants it to be."
— Teaching from Dharma

Don't you just hate it when you stub your toe on the corner of a coffee table?! As you hop around clutching your foot in agony, desperately trying to stumble onto the sofa, all the attention in your mind goes straight to your foot and the pain you're feeling. Then before you know it, you unleash a full-scale verbal and physical counterattack on the poor, defenceless, inanimate object.

In that moment, the pain you feel is real. It is your body's nervous system responding to an external stimulus, that if not acted on, would result in more pain and cause increasingly irreversible damage to your body. Pain is very useful for conditioning. If we touch a hot iron, we get scolded and so learn not to touch that part of the iron again. When we stub our toes on the coffee table time and time again, we learn to move more cautiously around that area. When you see people perform party tricks, like using a knife to stab the table between their fingers, they learn through pain avoidance where to stab and where not to stab. Their muscles become conditioned to only execute on the non-harmful actions.

Pain is useful and necessary to highlight our physical limitations, so we don't go overboard and end up killing ourselves. Suffering however, is all mental and mind constructed. Suffering is when your ego identifies with the pain. It is based in ego. Just like in the example with the coffee table, the pain comes from the physical collision with the foot and the table. The swelling, bleeding and bruising is all pain. This cannot be avoided. The suffering is the mental state we put ourselves in when we decide the event is negative and express it in a way that makes us feel significant.

In other words, the pain is real and useful, but the suffering is all ego based and doesn't have to exist. In the case of hitting your foot against the coffee table, as the blood rushes to that area, making it feel hot and throbbing, you could decide to not identify with that pain. Instead, you could look at it objectively and analyse the physical feeling in your body. By doing so you would remain in the present moment and would not identify with the pain. You could control your reactions and choose how to respond, rather than being swept away with emotion.

(**Experiment**: As a physical experiment, slowly pinch the skin above your triceps muscle. This area of the body is extremely sensitive. As you pinch this area with increasing intensity, practise staying present and witnessing your reaction. Just feel the pain and practise detaching your ego and any suffering from the experience. You should feel pain, but you should not cringe or feel sorry for yourself in any way. It should be an entirely observing, witnessing, accepting, and watching experience. Take caution when doing this as the pain can become very intense, very quickly, and stop if the pain becomes excessively intense.)

You may think the concept of detaching the pain from the suffering is difficult to do or understand. This is because it is a form of meditation. By being in the present moment, you take things in as they are, rather than manifesting a second meaning or back story behind it. You take the experience at face value, and there is nothing more or nothing less to it. By practising meditation frequently, you learn to live more in the here and now, rather than where a lot of people in the world live, inside their own heads.

Animals like cats or dogs live more in the present moment than we do, mainly because we have the ability to think things through and imagine future and past events. If we're always thinking of what we will do next, or of things that have happened in the past, it means we miss out on being fully present now and experiencing all that is going on around us. If you're a driver commuting from work to home, you have probably experienced forgetting the entire journey home, then snapping out of your daydream when you park up on your driveway. This is an example many of us have experienced that shows how easy it is to get distracted and stop being present.

Another way to think about it is by imagining walking your dog in the park. You have him on the lead and are walking towards a row of tall green trees whilst the sun sets behind them. When you see the sight of those tall green trees, you remember the time you were 8 years old, playing hide and seek with your school friends and hiding behind a similar tree. Boom! You are not present. You have let your focus slip. You have slid right out of reality and into your mind, where it is replaying a memory you had when you were 8 years old. Your dog on the other hand, only sees the sun setting behind the tall green trees and remains in the moment to experience this spectacular view.

This slipping of focus is the result of an untrained mind. When we practise meditation frequently, we strengthen our minds so we have more awareness and control of the thoughts running through them.

Amy and Tina work in sales and sit across the same

desk from one another. They get on well and often hang out for drinks after work. One Friday afternoon while they were both on sales calls, Amy looks over to Tina and sees her rolling her eyes right at her. Tina ends her call, but before Amy gets off the line, their boss calls Tina into his office to send her on the last sales meeting for the day.

Amy, still on the line to her client, is confused why Tina gave her that look. Gradually she becomes more introspective as to what she could have done to make Tina do that. She thinks of possible reasons but can't think of anything solid it could be. The thought lingers in her mind, stressing her out, leaving her unable to shake it off and move on. At 5:30pm everyone gets ready to head home. Tina did not return to the office and instead went straight home after her sales meeting finished, so Amy didn't get to see Tina and ask her if everything was ok.

Over the weekend Amy gets more confused. She hasn't received a text or call from Tina and refuses to send her one first. She figures if Tina has a problem with her, she should be the one to bring it up. She gets increasingly annoyed at Tina's lack of communication and starts to think she is being bitchy, childish, and overly sensitive.

Amy spends the weekend with her boyfriend's family and has a pleasant time, but at the back of her mind she can't help but think about Tina, and she regularly asks her boyfriend for advice over the matter.

Then by the time Monday comes around, Amy's pissed! As soon as she gets in the office, she marches right over to Tina and confronts her about it, demanding a reason why she had been so cold and reacted in such a way. Tina's surprised and confused, clearly not sure what Amy is going on about. Amy explains when the incident happened, and Tina disdainfully replied, "I was just adjusting my contact lenses you idiot."

With minimal effort our minds can slip into a state of anxiety and suffering. Simple miscommunication like this can cause countless arguments, failed relationships, wars, and even deaths in the world, and it all arises from a suffering state. A state that is mind manifested and not based on any truth. This is why the important practise of meditation, of being in the here and now and experiencing life as it actually is, is crucial for keeping the peace in this increasingly highly emotionalised world.

In the 1960s, to protest the persecution of Buddhists by the South Vietnamese Government, a Vietnamese monk by the name of Thích Quảng Đức, sat in a busy Saigon road intersection and had a man pour petroleum on him whilst he entered a deep state of meditation. Once the petroleum was poured, Thích Quảng Đức lit a match and his body was instantly engulfed in flames. He did not move. He did not scream. He did not show any signs of suffering.

As his body turned from a living man to a black charcoal figure, Thích Quảng Đức's body would have felt pain. However, his ability to control his mind allowed him to experience the event, but to seemingly not identify with the pain. Meaning, he was able to completely bypass the suffering he would have experienced, had he not been so absorbed into the moment.

Few people ever get to reach this level of self-mastery, but it is possible. Thích Quảng Đức's example was extreme and he had spent a large portion of his life mastering his power of focus to be able to successfully carry out such an act.

You may not need to dis-identify with the thoughts in your mind to this extent, however even having a fraction of Thích Quảng Đức 's ability, would allow you to become totally fearless in any challenge you'd want to overcome in your life.

FEAR OF REJECTION AND THE EGO

Fear of rejection is widely considered one of the biggest and most common fears people have. It is an important part of our internal and evolved wiring, as being rejected from the tribe meant being excluded from food, shelter, protection, and ultimately survival.

However, in today's modern revolutionised world, the chances of being rejected and banished outside of the tribe's territory is highly unlikely. Depending on the level of your resources and resourcefulness, you could pack up and leave one area to become just as successful and thrive in another area.

Now, in our more civilised society, what's more common is to be rejected in your sexual advances by someone you find attractive. Alternatively, a potential client could reject a deal or the opportunity of working with you. It could be having a job interviewer turn you down. Today, there are countless social and non-life-threatening situations you can be rejected by.

Being they are non-life-threatening means we should have no reason to fear. We know we can move to another location, find another job, build another peer group, or find another companion, and we can carry on living freely. However, the one thing that's life will be threatened is our ego.

Your ego is the collection of stories and past experiences you have been a part of, which over time has pooled together to form your sense of identity. Otherwise referred to and experienced as your 'self'. It is all the attributes related to a person when you think of their name. It is the soundtrack in your mind, the voice running behind every thought you have. It is not who you actually are deep down, but the ego shows up so consistently it

can be mistaken for your sense of self. Its use :
you understand and perceive things to give yoι
chance of survival.

Your ego represents your values and personality. It
contains your sense of morals and ethics that determine
how you think and act in life. It is your conscience. One
of your values may be, 'killing another person is bad'. This
is good for the world we live in, as it means you won't go
to prison and can enjoy living your life freely. Another one
of your values may be, 'being an attentive and curious
listener is good'. This can help you appreciate the
thoughts of another human being, which can be felt by
that person, allowing the pair of you to experience a
deeper, richer connection compared to others who prefer
talking over listening.

The thoughts and stories your ego most frequently
repeats conditions you to believe that that is who you are.
Your parents may have fearfully told you not to speak to
strangers thousands of times growing up. Hearing this,
combined with the feelings they evoked in us, conditions
us to believe in their highly emotionalised belief, that
'strangers are not to be trusted'. This is useful information
to hear as a child to remain safe, but later in life, when
you're in the business world and need to network and
establish trust with 'strange' connections, this
conditioning will work against you.

Hurting the ego is attacking its sense of identity. We
hurt the ego when we input a new story or belief that
contradicts the previous conditioning your ego has relied
on and repeatedly told itself. The only way to change the
egos identity is to frequently condition it with new stories.
Initially it will reject these new thoughts, but once it is
backed up with enough relevant reference experiences, it
will condition a new identity to take hold.

Humans are a never-ending work in progress. Since the dawn of man, our ego has been evolving and adapting with the times. Thousands of years ago, the threat of death was all around. Threats such as wars with other societies, lack of food, diseases, and bigger predators were more frequently experienced. With more threats around, the ego would have needed to work more for genuine survival purposes.

Just 200 years ago, the average life expectancy was less than 40 years old. We didn't have globalised industrial farming, mining, shipping, and other resources. Now, in some developed countries across the world, if we want anything we can hop onto Amazon and have it shipped to us in under 24 hours! Medicines and skilled surgeons can save lives much quicker and with more accuracy than past civilisations. A banana can be plucked from a tree in the Caribbean, and despite being thousands of miles away, it can be in our mouths in under 48 hours. Our huge jumps in technology have lengthened and improved the quality of human life significantly in a very short period of time. For developed countries, it is safe to say our basic needs can fairly easily be met.

We have developed so quickly our evolutionary wiring hasn't caught up to our current quality of life. So, despite this low-risk, long-life era in human history we have been lucky enough to be born into, our egos have continued working for our survival. However, with a lack of life-threatening situations to respond to, the ego now finds threatening situations in more social areas. This 'new' death is based around your identity and how you are seen by others, also known as your reputation.

With 'reputational death', we fret over every interaction and think about how we were perceived in it. We can obsess about what another person thought about what we did, how it made them feel, how it makes us look, and how they think about us. One after the other, an array of thoughts can arise out of a simple interaction that could have ended minutes, hours, weeks, years, or even decades ago. When we remember the specific event, we relive the experience and feel how we felt, evoking all the same emotions we experienced when the event actually happened. By doing so, it drives the original event deeper into our minds, adding more weight to the beliefs and stories we live our lives around.

This causes a 'them vs us' dynamic in our minds, which adds to our sense of identity and feeling of individuality. From this viewpoint we further analyse situations, judging ourselves and others, and in the process, we end up losing time and energy over imagined feelings that don't exist. Productivity goes down, we daydream over impossible scenarios, we get easily distracted, like missing our junction when driving, and all the while we are in a completely fictional mind state.

To become fearless in anything, silencing your ego is crucial. Your ego is just doing its best to keep you alive, but you're not in the tribe anymore. Challenging the tribe chief's authority could have led to banishment, leading to loneliness, a harder life, and a higher probability of an earlier death. Challenging your boss's ideas, by highlighting his errors and sharing a better alternative won't. You could experience feeling flushed, along with the common physical signs of fear, followed by a verbal smack on the wrist, and maybe a change in the energy dynamic of your relationship, but chances are you won't be killed over it.

Let's say you do lose your job over it, and he uses his wide influence to spread rumours about you, slandering your name to everyone in your town. You can still move.

I'm not saying not to fight, I'm just highlighting the fact that it's not as bad as it once was. Now you have the option to relocate and start afresh in almost any town, city, or country across the world. The choices are endless.

Other people's judgement of us keeps us from putting ourselves out there. We don't put our hand up in class to answer the question, in case we get it wrong and get publicly shamed. The opposite is also true, where if we answer the question correctly, we don't get labelled as a 'nerd' or 'teacher's pet'.

Flying under the radar is a strategy many people use to carry on living a meagre existence, hoping they don't attract attention and have the world see them for who they truly are. Perhaps they had shown their vulnerabilities in the past. Perhaps they had been mocked or belittled, and through a one-time event or continuous experiences, they learned to not express their fullest self, in case they open up too much and get rejected yet again.

But rejection is unavoidable in life. In fact, it is necessary. Rejection is needed for learning and growth to begin. By being rejected when pitching an idea, you learn to deliver a better pitch or to create a better offering. By being rejected by your crush, you learn what not to say next time, and it may set off a spark in you to learn to develop your personality more to be surer in yourself.

When it comes to what the mind fusses over, compared to the experience in reality, the mind can make things seem much worse, because of the ego playing out worst-case scenarios to help to protect you.

Silencing your ego is the first step to freedom. When you feel judgement, it is not your body feeling the judgement, it is just your mind and ego. Realise there is another level above the ego's relentless rambling. It is your true self. It is the silent, all seeing, all witnessing, all accepting mental state of being truly present and in the moment. In this state you can remain calm and act with clarity and certainty. The egos voice cannot rise to this level of awareness and in this state, fear cannot limit you.

EXPECTATIONS VS REALITY

Defining "Zen": Enlightenment by meditation in which there is no consciousness of self.

Living in reality is not as easy as you think. Most people live in the mental jumble of their thoughts and perspectives, giving little consideration to what is actually happening in any given situation. Information gets processed through their filters, which is control by their egos. This changes how they experience an event. A well-intentioned event could be well-received by one person but hated by another. Fights, divorces, and general misery can result from having different interpretations of something that actually happened, verses what someone expected to happen.

This misinterpretation of information goes back to the persons ego. As previously mentioned, the ego is a highly emotionalised entity. It filters all the information you receive during a day and registers the information that would either help you or harm you. However, before it has reached the point of being banked into your mind, the original piece of information gets altered to fit the capabilities of your ego. It takes the information, extracts what it wants out of it, giving it a specific meaning, and then it is stored in your mind, attached with the connotations your ego has given it.

This registering of information is useful as it gives the events and occurrences in our life meaning, priority, and importance, but fundamentally, it is fictional. It is information that has been accepted in a modified way, not in its original format. It doesn't take much to influence the ego. A side-angled glance, an accidental brush of shoulders, or a simple grammatical error has the power to challenge the ego and send it into a negative frenzy. As the resentment builds inside you, you can become totally convinced that a person you have known for your entire life has suddenly turned and wants to hurt you.

After work one evening, George comes home to see his wife, Claire, sitting on the sofa. Claire has had a great day. At work she submitted the reports she needed to get done on time, she tidied up the house once she got back from work, and now she settles down to watch her latest favourite Netflix shows.

George, on the other hand, has had a less than productive day. With the stress of his work deadlines hanging over his head, the pressure inside him gets higher and higher. If that wasn't bad enough, he just got cut off on the motorway whilst heading home and got into an argument with the other driver. And to top it all off... it's been raining! What a day!

George has been looking forward to the highlight of his day, which would be when he gets to see his wife. He can't wait to kiss Claire, allowing all the troubles of the day to melt away. He envisions running upstairs, getting into his jammies, cracking open a bottle of wine, and spending some quality time with his lovely partner.

However, when he comes in, he sees Claire just sitting there engrossed in the show. Claire is so captivated that she doesn't take the time to pause the show to greet him, stirring up feelings of insignificance in him, proceeding in George losing his shit.

Like a kid in a supermarket who doesn't get what he wants, George throws all his toys out the stroller, in this case his umbrella and work bag, and begins yelling at Claire. A fight ensues and Claire gets annoyed, as this is clearly not her doing, and realises George is using her as a verbal punching bag. Claire shouts back, both George and

Claire go to separate ends of the house, and no love is shared between them that night.

George was expecting understanding, attention, and affection. He was met with none of these attributes.

Another possibility could be, George comes home, gets mad at Claire, but Claire is more aware than usual in this moment. She observes him quietly and when he finishes with his frustrated rant, she says, "I know this isn't about me. Sit here, let's talk about it. What is this really about?" By not retaliating and instead just hearing his ranting, Claire can observe George is frustrated with something. She can then remain present and attentive, rather than feeling victimised and becoming equally aggressive and reactive.

All the while this is happening, a fly is on the wall just looking at them both. It is merely observing with no emotional attachment, just aware of its environment. If it senses a threat it moves away, and if not, it stays put just doing what it needs to do to survive another day of being a fly. It is totally present and reacts to them in the moment appropriately.

In the latter example of George and Claire's relationship dynamic, Claire held a reality-based position. Her focus was in the here and now, so she was able to react accordingly from a free state of mind, unattached to her mental position, which would have made her react in a more emotionally charged and confrontational way. From this state, she has clarity with her thoughts and can assess the situation accordingly. She can provide structure and direction to the interaction, which can be aimed at the greater good, leading to both George and Claire experiencing a lovely evening together.

In the former, George held an expectation-based position. He was trying to control things outside of his control. This is fighting a losing battle, as you can never fully know how people will act. The only thing you can control in your life is the actions you choose to partake in. Everything else is uncontrollable. From an expectation-based mental state, it is certain you will experience a differing reality. The expectation in the mind is almost always a perfectly executed fantasy of how things could go. It doesn't take a genius to know things will never be as perfect as we want them to be. To believe so is naïve and immature.

Then we have the fly. This creature lives with Zen-like awareness in the present moment. For the fly there is no such thing as time. It remains completely aware of everything around it. It has no consciousness of its 'self'. It has no identity, mental limits, or emotions about itself. It is incapable of suffering as it has no emotions. It only lives in the moment and acts accordingly. It just is. This can be a difficult concept to grasp, but practising meditation and becoming more Zen-like will allow us to live less stressful, less depressed, happier, more engaging, passionate, and purposeful lives.

THE "WHAT IF" PARADIGM

The ego will always try to protect its host against information that conflicts with its built-up identity. We must learn to become more in tune with reality than reacting to things that clash with our egos. By doing so, we can become more compassionate and have more understanding for other human beings. We could relate with others better because we are not tied up in our own issues. Instead we can be more attentive to them, and we can have greater control of the emotions and thoughts running through our own minds.

This is all well and good in theory, but humans are notorious for having spiralling thoughts. A thought can start off small, but can expand quickly, taking up more mind space and blocking our ability to think and act rationally. We continually fret, thinking about things that could attack our sense of identity or our physical state of being, which could lead to the death of a part of our identity, or our physical death.

Whether in a family, office, class or a general social environment, we want to feel valued and respected. Significance, credibility, and being taken seriously, are all feelings the ego relishes. So, when someone cuts down our ideas, we obsess. Our minds can spiral out of control, from thoughts of revenge, to causing physical harm to that person. We can end up categorising their entire personality from witnessing only one of their actions. We may question their backgrounds, their parents, and how they were raised, which in doing so puts us in a mental state of superiority.

When we think of past and future events, our minds often replay either the best-case or worst-case scenarios. With best-case scenarios, you may think you can achieve your goals with optimism alone. As if everything you do is flawless, nothing is out of place, no issues arise, you just execute on a golden path. With worst-case scenarios, your fears are grossly exaggerated. You self-induce a fear frenzy, stopping yourself from rationally functioning as your mind worries. The thing is, it never works out how it is in our minds. Whether it is a euphoric victory or an apocalyptic ending, it never plays out like that in real life. In reality, the daily humdrum of life is quite monotonous. The events in life never stray too far from the incessant equilibrium of daily living.

The stock market crashes, and in our minds, we think about our economies collapsing, all the power shutting down and having to live in a Mormon-like state of living, where everyone chips in to help everyone else. Or, on the other end of the spectrum, we end up living in selfish, wretched, criminalised communities, where after a busy day of killing and looting, we gather around burning cars and oil drums to keep warm as the night closes in.

However, in reality, we talk about it around the water cooler at work, we go back home, watch TV, cook, eat, and go to sleep, waking up to live another day where we react and adapt to every situation we encounter. When it's all said and done, we end up just getting on with it and carrying on living. It's always better or worse from our ego's perspective.

News outlets and various forms of media plug into our inherent desire and involuntary urge to know what is happening around us. Our constant search for threats is relentless for the sake of our survival. News and media companies exploit this innate trait in us by continuously pumping out new stories that keep us gripped to their channels. Then we talk about it further with our peers and loved ones, further spreading the messages into our societies. Being clued up and having this knowledge first makes our egos feel significant when sharing it with others. We then add our own opinions on the situation, which drives the issue deeper within us. As a combination of hearing it from media sources, and our own self-perpetuated conversations with others, we develop very strong feelings and beliefs about issues we initially had no connection to.

After sharing some content, I connected with a lady on Facebook, let's call her 'Jill'. Jill is in her 50s and has a husband and kids. She has a good job, which allows her to live a comfortable life. We spoke about the jobs and careers we had, our family's, life in our separate countries, and I asked her about where she had travel to in the world. She mentioned a few places within the USA, but she hadn't left North America.

Life being short is an understatement. Our planet is huge. Even if we had 10 lifetimes, we couldn't see all of what the world has to offer. The mystery and history of the pyramids in Egypt, the majesty of the Taj Mahal in India, the rich history and culture in the UK, the northern lights in Greenland, the beauty of the Caribbean and thousands of other places are so accessible today, now more than ever. We can fly around the planet in less than 24 hours, which was simply impossible less than 100 years ago. We have such an incredible resource at our disposal. All we need to do is go online, book a flight, accommodation, and turn up. For those who can afford to, it has never been easier or cheaper. But when I asked Jill why she hadn't left the USA, and why she didn't even want to, her reply was, "It's too dangerous. I don't trust others".

Unfortunately, Jill isn't the exception. Countless thousands of people who could live internationally adventurous lives don't, partly due to news and media programming. Televised fear-inducing programming mentioning wars, terrorism, rioting, rapes, murders, and other forms of negativity flood the audience's minds. Graphic images and sounds deliver enough sensory information to log a threat within the mind, in relation to the place of the incident. Further highlighting that the area they live in must be 'safe' in comparison. People then take special precautions not to go near the reported area and instead live in an imaginary state of security around their home and local comforts. When in fact, any form of crime or disaster could happen right on their doorstep.

The messages in the media are all around us and relentless. Chances are, as you go along your normal commute to work, you will see a headline or advertisement designed to induce fear within you. If it happens to be relevant to you, it can pique your curiosity enough to want to learn more. It's in our nature to seek out threats to our identity and physical existence. If you don't stand guard, any persistent subtle messaging can easily creep into your mind. Before long, you can unconsciously begin repeating and spreading the messages to others, saying things like, "Don't go there, XYZ happened there". Or, "Did you hear about XYZ? Be careful, see if you can avoid it if you can". Or, "Watch out, our kind of people aren't welcome around there".

With little thought, we can pass these media-based fears onto our children and future generations, by sharing stories that have no relevance to us, other than to limit our thinking and actions in some way. Our children, instead of growing up curious and wanting to discover, can grow up discouraged and fearing the same things we have learned to fear. Our blind acceptance of the medias programming and our certainty when sharing it, further reinforces the messages to those who we have an easy influence over. Eventually, we boil it down to a quick phrase that can be unconsciously repeated hundreds of thousands of times over a lifetime, like "take care", or "stay safe", or "be careful", whilst not paying attention to how this subtle conditioned phrase affects ourselves or others.

It goes without saying, there is helpful information broadcasted in the media that does affect you and the entire nation you live in. In the beginning of 2020, an outbreak of COVID-19, a type of virus in the Coronavirus family that causes respiratory symptoms in humans, spread throughout the world. Countries locked their borders. People were told to stay at home, to not infect others and slow the spread of the virus. In many countries across the world, all non-essential businesses and jobs were stopped in order to limit the pandemic. At the time of this writing, hundreds of thousands of people have been infected. Tens of thousands of people have died. It is predicted the peak of the outbreak has yet to be reached, and as of now, the definitive cure does not exist. The statistics and facts associated to such events are definitely 'newsworthy' to keep the population notified about major developments related to their survival. In the final section of this book, we discuss what you can do when in truly life-threatening situations.

However, what we are discussing here is the irrelevant news you wouldn't have known about in your entire lifetime, unless it was shown to you via major broadcasting. It's sad when someone gets killed in a car accident, or in a gang-related crime over 100 miles away from us, but had it not been for major broadcasting, we would remain blissfully unaware of it. It would not have affected our perception of the world or given us a sense of paranoia about specific demographics or locations.

The 'What If Paradigm' keeps us in its control by making us seek out future threats, so we never fully live in and appreciate the moment. Our minds come up with situations that we can work out how to avoid. We think thoughts like, "What do I do if while I'm lying on this beach a Tsunami happens and I'm defenceless?" An unsure driver may think, "I need to see my Aunt today, but doing so means I would need to take the motorway and risk getting into an accident with a fast driver, so I'd better take public transport instead, even if it is an hour longer than driving". A new employee may think, "I know I need to give this presentation in front of people today, but I'm scared of losing focus and not doing a good job, so I'll get someone else in my team to do my part instead".

I must admit, whenever I fly, on takeoff or landing, I can imagine every possible worst-case scenario. I imagine the plane not having enough thrust after taking off and so nose diving into the ground. On landing, if there is any turbulence upon arrival, my mind is flooded with thoughts of quickly sending a text to my family to tell them I love them, just before the plane smashes into the runway. I grip the arm rests and drive my feet into the floor, but what takes me out of this fearful state is looking around me. Seeing things as they are. Realising I am in the moment. I look at the people around me, perhaps in their own fearful state. I look at the small vibrations the plane makes when coming down to land. I look at my hands, which is a great way for me to come back to reality. I continuously practise being in the present moment to eliminate any feelings of fear.

The 'What if paradigm' robs us of the moment and keeps our mind in a perpetual state of reacting to an imagined threat, even if that threat never actually comes.

FEAR OF SUCCESS

Fear's job is to hold you back and stop you from doing something. But when going after success, this is counterproductive. Many times, having the courage to take action, despite feeling fear, is the deciding factor between succeeding or failing.

On the journey to success, it's guaranteed you would run into failure along route. Embracing this early on is key to liberating yourself. Knowing failure is inevitable in some shape and form allows you to look for it and be more optimistic once it eventually comes. Failure is a part of success. Without failing you wouldn't know how to navigate pitfalls, you wouldn't learn anything that could transform your life, and you couldn't appreciate the success if the win came so easily. You would take things for granted and become entitled. Your judgement would become clouded and your ego would be over-inflated.

We see successful people in the news or on social media and desire for their lifestyle, but we forget that what we see now is the accumulation of many failed attempts. As we couldn't see their 'struggle' or 'rise to success', we assume they were just destined to be on our screens. Even with those who succeed from their first attempt, we do not get to see their life whilst growing up. Their parents could have conditioned them from very early on with positivity which spread throughout their lives, accumulating in good connections and resourcefulness that helped to propel them into success on their first try. For most people who 'make it', we don't see their previous attempts that crashed and burned. We don't see the Oscar winning actor on previous auditions getting turned down repeatedly as they honed their craft. We don't see the billionaire who launched business after business, becoming broke in the process, until he worked on the idea that made his wealth. We don't see the greatest boxer of all time in the gym for 8 hours a day, developing their technique and doing tedious footwork drills. We see them as the overnight celebrity, but we don't see the years or decades of work that brought them to where they are now. Many people avoid failure at all costs, but without failing regularly, life would be very boring and mediocre at best.

Discipline is a heavily under-utilised skill for many people. If people had the discipline to cook their meals for the week on Sunday evening, they could free up an hour each evening instead of cooking. They could cook themselves healthier meals rather than picking up fast food, and they can control the size of each portion so they don't overindulge. This would lead to a healthier body, increase the length of their lives, save them money, and help them look and feel better.

If people committed to going to the gym just 3 days a week, for example, every Sunday morning, Tuesday evening after work, and Thursday evening after work, they would feel healthier from week one. They would lose fat, strengthen their bones and muscles, look sexier, and also be a good influence on the people around them, indirectly helping others in the process.

If people dedicated an hour each night after they finish their jobs to find a passion or work on an idea to become financially free, in a matter of months or years they could be able to live independently. They could be in control of their lifestyle and not wake up dreading each day they spend working a job where they feel unfulfilled.

Despite sounding contradictory, being disciplined frees people. When actions and behaviours become habitual and automatic, your brain is free to think about other things that could help you. Once habits like your exercise programme and food intake are automatic, it will only be a matter of time before you get the body you desire and the vitality to go after more challenging pursuits.

When you set up a plan for a business idea or a strategy to become financially free, all you would need to do is simply execute on the daily tasks that would get you there. As challenges appear, you find a way to resolve them and execute again. Eventually, the payoff will come, and you would have the income and time to do more of the things you love. Being disciplined in one area can lead to freedom in other areas. Once you build your wealth, you then have unlimited time to spend with your family, travel, and explore all your interests.

Discipline is your best friend when going after anything outside of your reach in life. By persistently taking manageable steps of action, no goal, despite how audacious, is unattainable. Action + Time = Results. The secret is consistency. Taking action consistently is key in getting ideas off the ground and to have long-term results. Sometimes chasing the results can lead to frustration and quitting. Instead, focus on finding a process you enjoy doing. Find something about the pursuit that you can fall in love with and makes you want to get to it each day. It may take some trial and error, and some ideas may need to be cut, but by never giving up, it will only be a matter of time until you are on the right path.

Sometimes, even with a supportive family, your ideas or desires in life can get thwarted. Naturally, the people around you want you to fit in, but they may not understand the motivation or reasoning for your plans. This could make or break a lot of people. The drive is towards their goals and dreams, but they have been heavily programmed with family standards. They could have been subtly conditioned to put family first, to have to attend all family events without question, to not speak out, to push their desires down, and do what's best for everyone rather than just themselves.

Fear of missing out (FOMO) is powerful, but when it comes to your success, missing out on some things is simply inevitable. You have to sacrifice some things to achieve other things. If you want a hot-bod with a chiselled six-pack but don't want to give up drinking with the boys every Friday and Saturday night, followed by unhealthy food to nurse yourself better over the weekend, your dreams of having a beach body won't be realised.

If after work, you unwind by watching TV, followed by dinner, dessert, and more TV, with no time dedicated for working out, you'd better get comfortable having a gut bulging out of you. It's good to realise that the leisurely things you don't want to miss out on, are most likely counterproductive in getting you closer to your goals and dreams. It's better to flip it around, whereby missing out on taking consistent action towards your goals and dreams gives you the same sense of FOMO.

You can help yourself take productive actions more easily by increasing the amount of friction needed to do leisurely activities, like turning on the TV, or eating bad food. Alternatively, you could decrease the amount of friction needed to work out or get on your computer and put in some work towards your future. Simple steps like taking the battery out of the remote control or unplugging the TV after every use can add steps of friction towards watching TV. This makes you more aware of turning on the device and gives you the time to reconsider and do something more productive. By having your fridge stocked full of fresh foods, you are more likely to cook wholesome meals rather than chucking a frozen pizza in the oven. If you wanted a pizza, it would mean you would have to walk or drive to the store and get the item before you would even start to cook it. This adds friction to the process by deterring you from the unhealthy food and makes you want to choose the more convenient route of cooking at home instead.

By making habits of the actions needed to attain your goals, you come closer to living the life you always desired. When it comes down to going for your goals, a decision must be made:

> ➢ Are other people's opinions of me more important than my happiness?
> ➢ Which will I regret more, living to please others, or pursuing my interests?
> ➢ Which will fulfil me more, falling in line to other's expectations of me, or expressing myself and living with integrity?

At a certain point, perhaps after much internal confliction, a line in the sand must be drawn. Taking all emotion out of the situation, a logical decision to do what needs to be done for the sake of your happiness and satisfaction must be executed on. Providing you don't break bridges with people and always treat them respectfully, when your success is attained, hopefully they are supportive and proud of you. However, if they are not, realise they may be discontent with their lives. It may shine a light on their lack of ambition, or that they never had the courage to pursue and make their dreams a reality. It may make them feel as if they wasted their time, they may not have had the resources or been resourceful enough, they may have simply given up, or they may just be envious assholes.

At the end of the day, you have to sleep with yourself.

As you lay your head on the pillow for the day, only you know how hard you went at going for the things you want to achieve. If you didn't, you, and only you, get to swallow that pill. The more often you swallow that pill, the more normal it becomes, and the more your ambitions weaken. You 'settle'. You'll justify and persuade yourself that what you're doing is normal and fine, but when you look back on your life, you will know you had given up in some way. When it's too late, and you don't have the time and energy to go after things that you could have done when you were more able, that will be a feeling you will have to live with. Perhaps turning into a grumpy old man or woman, pissed at the smallest things not going your way, because you couldn't attain the life you wanted, when you could do something about it.

Other people don't hold us back. We hold ourselves back. Saying "No" to others is the first step in getting our time back for ourselves. Other people will not get us the life we desire. Our lives are our responsibilities, and achieving our desires is the result of independent thought and action.

Regarding attaining success, the hip-hop artist Snoop Dogg was recorded describing 'The Gap'. He explained, as you go for any kind of success in life, you have to begin to do things that will help to elevate you. Your society may not understand, but all you need to know is you start at your base level, say level 1, and you want to increase several levels up, say level 10. As you are at level 1, it's likely the people around you are also at level 1. As you start to take actions that will elevate you to higher levels, it can inspire the people around you to also build their lives. All you know is you want to get to level 10 and won't stop until you get there. Now what will happen is, if they want to, they can also start increasing their levels, but if they choose not to, and are content staying at level 1 in life, an increasingly expanding 'gap' will appear.

The tension of this' gap' could cause issues with the people who are being 'left behind', but all you are doing is fulfilling your potential and choosing the path of realising your ambition.

EXTERNAL VALIDATION VS INTERNAL VALIDATION

Relying on others to set your course in life is risky business. Despite how concerned they are, or how much they love and care for you, they don't have your gut. They don't have your passion, your drive, your energy, or your vision. They only see things from their perspective. Even when you explain it to them, the message can become distorted by their experiences and filters, so they interpret it as a slightly different version of what you described. They may have your best interests at heart, but they can't take your journey for you.

Feeling important is a powerful motivator for many people. We want to share our ideas with others so they can appreciate our brilliance and give us a gratifying pat on the back, but if we become dependent on this, and it doesn't come, we could question our whole process and doubt our ideas strength. Relying on a strong internal compass is by far the best way to go about executing on your ideas.

This doesn't mean you never listen to anyone else. It means, after you have researched and learned as much as you feel is enough, only you have the final decision.

The way to build a strong internal compass is through experience. Through failing and succeeding in your efforts to achieve your goals, you develop the intuition needed to help you get to your desired outcomes. Failure and being vulnerable are part of the process towards achieving your goals. Nothing risked is nothing gained. The alternative is living such a careful life, where you know every step and how it will play out because you are playing it safe, but end up bored out of your skull, frustrated and miserably unfulfilled.

Taking the time to develop your internal compass is crucial for a fulfilling life. Without it, you become easy to influence and end up using your energy to advance the causes of others who have more control over their mindsets.

External validation is a path to insecurity and misery as you attempt to clamber after praise and acceptance from others to make you feel good about the things you do. Your internal compass is where happiness, fulfilment, and peace come from. Following your internal compass helps you to act in the direction of your values and beliefs. Once it is strong enough, nothing can tear it down. You are responsible for its strength, and the only way to strengthen it is by purposefully listening to and acting on your gut instincts.

GOOD FEARS

When you think of good fears to have, what comes to mind?

Falling?
Loud noises?
Physical threats?
Isolation?
Something that has the power and ability to overwhelm you?
Lack of food?
Death?

It is normal if most of these things could send you into a fear state. Our fear of falling keeps us away from standing too close to the edge of cliff tops and makes us want to back away. Our fear of loud noises helps us to locate possible dangers and get us going in the opposite direction. Our fear of physical threats helps us not to have our skin and internal organs pierced by weapons, teeth, or claws, and so keeps us alive. Our fear of isolation keeps us in groups so we can look out for one another and keeping socially active helps to prevent our minds from deteriorating. Our fear of starvation keeps us working and earning money to put food in our bellies. These fears are inherent fears. We need to have peace of mind over these things, otherwise we would physically die. It is useful having such fears as without them our lives would be short and painful.

However, if these are the main things to fear, why do we feel fear in so many other situations. Why is it that when an employee is in the boardroom and about to deliver a pitch to their managers, they freeze up and can't string a simple sentence together?

The irrational fears we experience on a day-to-day basis are typically felt when we are conscious of other people's reactions to how we think and act. Our desire to fit in with the crowd that would best protect and serve us is now our main priority.

Whilst growing from a child to an adult, our free expression gradually gets reigned in, so over time, we turn into a generally generic cookie cut out of a human. One that fits into and functions how our society largely accepts.

But when it comes to creativity, expression, and creating something bigger than ourselves, this limited self is simply not powerful enough to bring about change and lasting impact in the world, or within leadership roles. At this point, a shedding of limitations is needed. This is a conscious effort to deprogram yourself from the internal dialogue of mainstream society and wake up to the freedom that's available for us all.

It's usually experienced by a sudden realisation that things could be better or done differently, typically followed by a longer period of time to reach results. The reason it can take longer to get results is because reprogramming yourself to the new mission can require a number of affirming experiences and thoughts. Over time, this saturates the mind, adding weight to the new beliefs, and overpowers the previously held beliefs.

Additionally, the influence of the people around you and the messaging in the media constantly program you with their beliefs. This is why people who become more fearless and go for what they want in life tend to avoid contact with others who are not going in the same direction as they are, as having to convince themselves is tough enough. Having someone else who is constantly questioning, picking apart, and making you defend your ideas is exhausting. This effort could be put into the projects that need the time and energy to get an idea off the ground, from the mind into reality.

So rather than being consumed by fear, how can we use it to help us get what we want in life?

SECTION 2:
REFRAMING FEAR

All that has been covered in the previous section is enough for you to go out in the world and live fearlessly. Simply having the awareness of what fear is and what it does to you can stop it from limiting you. Knowing how and why it conjures up feelings in the body allows you to recognise its process, and in doing so, you become present enough for the fear to be overcome. You can detach your emotions and identity from the fear and rationally move forward.

Visualise it as a two-storey house. Your thoughts and fears are like a torrent of water flooding the ground floor. When you are on the ground floor, you are too busy being swept up by the current and end up reacting to everything around you. Here you identify with your thoughts. You experience them as if they are who you are. Your thoughts will never stop coming in. Control of the mind here is limited. When you are on the 1st floor landing, looking at the water flooding the house below, you are aware of your thoughts. You are not in the midst of experiencing them. You are high and dry. You have not identified with your thoughts and can witness them with a degree of detachment. You are in a position where you would not get swept away by the waves of thought. You see everything as it is. You are present and in the moment. You are in the fearless state.

You could put this book down now. This is enough. But next we will uncover more about how to reframe fear and make fear your bitch. How to purposefully control it, and how to use it to your advantage.

"He who has overcome his fears will truly be free"
- Aristotle

OVERCOMING FEAR

There are two main routes to overcoming your fears: a 'this is enough' moment, or through conditioning. As with the title, the 'this is enough' moment is when you've reached a point where you are sick and tired of reacting in the same fearful way towards the stimulus. You realise a change is needed, and you instinctually revolt against whatever was limiting you by taking action in a major or minor way. Examples could be sticking up for yourself against the school bully, the demanding boss, or the abusive husband. Their relentless provoking and taunts finally hit your breaking point, where you refuse to stand for any more of their attempts to control you. You get fired up and fight back, for better or worse, because your integrity is in full effect and you exercise your right to command respect for yourself. In a split second, you jump onto a new trajectory for that area of your life.

After having an experience like this, you may also experience higher levels of confidence towards confronting other fears in your life. By knowing you can conquer one fear, you also know it is possible to keep challenging other fears, subsequently breaking down all the limiting thoughts and behaviours that held you back from going for the things you want in life. The memory of the 'this is enough' moment, is then brought up when confronted with new fears. It reminds you that you have the power to step right over the new fears, and not let them drain and disempower you.

The conditioned route to overcoming fears is also as it states. This path is more systematic in its approach. It requires diligently taking steps to reduce the fear over time. It involves collecting reference experiences that pool together to form the basis of confidence for the individual. It works in a similar way to traditional balance scales, in that on the left side, there is the weight of years of limited thinking and fear-based experiences. On the right side, there is an empty plate, yet to have any positive and affirming experiences added onto it. The more positive and fear-busting experiences you add to the right side, the heavier it becomes, thereby increasing its impact on the mind of the person being conditioned. Once the scales have tipped and the confident-thinking side becomes heavier than the fear-thinking side, the person becomes conditioned to be more expressive in that area of their lives.

An example here could be public speaking. Rarely does anyone start out as a great speaker. Usually in the beginning they refuse to speak in front of people, followed by being forced to do it, followed by stumbling through a speech, followed by the pain of being laughed at and made to feel like they're not cut out for it. Then once they get several talks in, they build their confidence and they start to ad-lib. Then instead of the full script, they bring bullet point notes to their talks to remind them to keep on track. Then they scrap the bullet points and just talk about their topic for the length of their speech. Until finally, they build up so much confidence in their speaking abilities, and the scales tip over so completely to their expressive side, that the only way to get them off stage is to ask the sound engineer to slowly mute their microphone and increase the backing music until they get the hint.

More on conditioning later in this section.

WRITING DOWN AND QUESTIONING YOUR FEARS

To eradicate fear, a higher level of thinking is required. It requires objective thinking. This type of thinking takes you to a mentally superior place, above your thoughts and emotions, where you can remove your identity from the situation. It is a solely present and attentive mental state of being.

One way to do this is by writing down the fear. This is similar to the reason we write a shopping list, so that when we go to the store and buy what we need, we don't get home only to realise we forgot the milk. By writing down the fear, we become more aware of what our fears are. Then, when they arise, we aren't as easily surprised and swept into emotionally reacting. The awareness of our fear allows us to prepare and rehearse for situations that cause us to feel fear. It also takes the sting and punch out of the fear. When we know what our fear is, we are better able to handle and deal with it appropriately.

Imagine there are two boxes with a snake in each box. Both boxes contain equally venomous snakes. One person attempts to reach inside the first box and gets bitten. This person would now panic, and rightly so. He doesn't know what type of snake it is, its potency, whether the venom would kill him, whether he would need to amputate his arm off, cause him to black out, or whether he would just feel drunk for a few hours. As he doesn't know what would happen, he thinks the worst and runs off in a panic to find someone who can help him survive. Another person opens the other box, reaches inside and also gets bitten. But this person knows what snake it is, how potent its venom is, how his body will react, and what he can do to counteract the effects of the poisonous bite.

He has more awareness of the situation and knows he can afford to spend some time looking at the snake, appreciating its beauty, feeling its scales, and marvelling at its fangs before dealing with the bite. He is less worried as he is more aware of the situation and so has more control of his emotions.

By writing down the fear and objectively thinking about it, the same level of curiosity can be applied to inspecting the fear, understanding it, learning about it, and overcoming it with logical good old-fashioned reasoning.

Writing down what you fear helps to free your consciousness from the anarchy that goes on inside your mind. There are a lot of thoughts flooding your mind in every minute of every day. Before you know it, so many things need to be done, and they continue stacking up. Without a list of some form to organise your thoughts, it is almost certain that tasks will get missed and buried in the relentless ramblings of the mind.

"A short pencil beats a long memory"
- Unknown

Now that your fears are written down somewhere, you may see how pathetic the fear was, how irrational it was, and how easy it is to stop that train of thinking. Some fears may be deep-rooted and may require more effort, but a lot of the smaller fears can be completely wiped out by using this short and easy technique.

Put yourself in the shoes of a parent. Imagine having your child come up to you and worriedly tell you some of the fears you wrote down. How would you explain to them it is nothing to be feared? How would you react to them saying such irrational fears? What steps would you take to help them get over their fears? Write down your answers next to each fear on your list. Use this technique to become mentally stronger and superior to your fears by dealing with them as a rational adult would.

After writing down your fears, you can prioritise them to the level of fear they induce in you and deal with them one by one. Start with the fears of least impact to you. Use them to build your confidence towards the bigger fears and systematically work to eliminate all the fears you hold in your mind.

For the deep-rooted fears that aren't overcome by just writing them down, asking questions to understand why you fear them is the next step in overcoming them. Ask questions such as: Why am I feeling fear towards this situation? What specifically do I fear most about it? Is this fear rational or irrational? How have I previously been conditioned in my life to feel fear in this situation? Your aim is to investigate the fear, so you understand why you experience it. By purposefully learning as much as you can about it, you see it for what it is, from an accurate and emotionally detached perspective. The only way to overcome a fear is to dis-identify from it and take it apart, to see how mentally manufactured it actually is.

LIMITING BELIEFS VS EMPOWERING BELIEFS

All beliefs are bullshit. They are all fiction-based. They are built from your experiences and from the words of others around you. You were born as a blank canvas, and from the moment you popped out into the world, you had bucket loads of other people's beliefs thrown all over you. This could be from the people closest to you, to a conversation you overheard in the street, to the advertisers who plant their messages on billboards all around the world. Beliefs are not based in reality. They are created and nurtured to support the decisions and lifestyle of a group of people. Just in case you missed it, they are not real!

This applies to everything. Let's keep it simple. Imagine your partner saying, "You're the best boyfriend in the world". She may believe it, but can it really be measured? For the sake of it, let's say it could. Chances are someone else is an even better partner in a relationship somewhere else around the world, making her statement redundant. She may experience a greater feeling of love towards you than her past relationships, but to say you are 'the best in the world' at something without any evidence is simply false. Sorry mate…

Now let's take sports teams. People can get so passionate about cheering after people who have no relation to them, as they run up and down a big rectangle, and attempt to put a ball of some kind into a net of some kind. Emotions fly high as people cry, cheer, laugh, and get infuriated by the actions of the two teams they are there to see. One fan believes their team is the greatest. Another fan on the other side of the stadium also believes their team is the best. Then one team ends up winning and the losing team's fans believe something went wrong. Perhaps they did their 'lucky' morning routine in the wrong order and it cost the team the game. Perhaps it's because it was an away game, and at home is where the team really perform at their best. Perhaps the team didn't need that win to stay in the league, so it doesn't really matter this time anyway. A bunch of other bullshit beliefs arise to justify their team losing the game. When in reality, they just got beaten by the better team that day. The figures and results are tangible, the belief is not. The winning team's fans go home and are in a state of euphoria for the rest of the day and can last for weeks. The losing team's fans are in dismay, walking home with their head in their hands. The level of belief from both team's fans could come from their location to the team's grounds, or because their parents liked those teams, so now it's 'tradition' to support them. Perhaps they are holding onto past success, and now this is their year to prove to the world they will come back on top.

Either way their belief in their teams are totally fictitious and are not based on any truth. A team's true worth relies on factors a fan cannot control. The fans belief is a personal, emotional connection to some aspect of the team. Had they had different life experiences, perhaps they were born elsewhere, or their family preferred different sports, they would be completely detached to the team.

How about politics? No one knows the exact outcome of voting for the parties they vote for. Once the party gets elected, the policies may change and not be put into effect as accurately as initially stated. But the belief in the leaders representing the parties, and the feelings they give people, is why many people vote for and stay loyal to them. For some it may be because their family and friends have always voted for a specific party, and they believe by voting for the same party, they will remain on good terms with their loved ones.

And what about religion? There are tens, if not hundreds of religions in the world today. Each has their methods to bring people to enlightenment and to a hope of an afterlife, but no one knows if there is a God. No one knows if what we do is for any reason at all. There has been no solid proof of the almighty creator, but we convince ourselves there must be something, even though all the evidence shines a light on there being no explanation.

Humans find great comfort in beliefs. We mould our lives around beliefs that are close to us, we move closer to places where are beliefs are stronger, but it is all fictitious. A belief is simply a thought you have repeated with strong emotion. You decide that is the way things are, and that is what you believe to be true, whether it helps you or harms you.

Now, if you're one of the people who haven't been offended and put this book down by now, here's the part where you can take control of your beliefs and create new beliefs to help you change your life.

By accepting all beliefs are bullshit, you can use this knowledge to create your own bullshit beliefs that better serve you. You can choose beliefs that help you become the person you want to be, rather than thoughtlessly accepting all the beliefs put on you by others.

Beliefs about yourself are created in 3 ways: by your experiences, what you hear others say, and the thoughts you say to yourself. Beliefs are transferred to others in 3 ways: words, voice inflexion, and body language. Beliefs are a powerful force in human nature. Beliefs are either limiting or empowering.

Limiting beliefs are thoughts that stop you and make you question whether you should be doing what you set out to do. An example would be: "I'm afraid of being seen as stupid by others". It's easy to see how this belief could make a person hesitant and fearful of freely expressing themselves in front of other people. Perhaps this person's biggest dream was to become a movie star. Having this belief would stomp out any chance of this person merely attempting auditions, thereby limiting the person from attaining their true potential, and can leave them with a taste of regret that could last a lifetime.

Empowering beliefs are thoughts that encourage and energise you to take on challenges. They can create determination in you to turn your desires into reality. An empowering belief of the previous example could be: "I care about my opinion of myself more than how others think of me. I don't want to live with regret, so I give my all towards anything I want to achieve." This belief would inspire a person to be vulnerable and put themselves out there to their fullest. They would be freer and more confident with their performance because their worth is not dependent on whether they get criticised or commended.

Empowering beliefs give people the hope and confidence needed to achieve the things they set out to achieve. The person with more empowering beliefs on their side can achieve bigger goals in life. It allows you to dream bigger, and gives you hope you could actually reach some of your goals. It's powerful enough to make you eagerly look forward to new fears arising, as you're convinced you can learn from them and know you could overcome them.

A final note on beliefs and one that is hugely impactful: hang around others with empowering beliefs and avoid those who spread limiting beliefs.

Have you ever met someone, who when they enter a room, the lights start to dim? Positive-energy vampires, sucking the life out of the room with their pessimism. It's a chore being around them. They bring others down and make them feel like, 'what's the point of doing anything?'. Those so negative it makes you want to stop hanging around them. These people may be all around you in your daily encounters. The trick is to avoid these people. Every now and then you will have to interact with 'one' but try to limit time with them as much as possible. The people who exhibit this behaviour could be the closest people in your life. It's hard to disassociate with these people but limiting time with them is the best cure for those you have close relationships with. With people you rarely see, it is very easy to cut them out of your life entirely. Your mind is a very susceptible place for thoughts of all kinds, positive and negative. Similar to the 'weighing scales analogy' as mentioned earlier, the mind will accept deposits from all sources within ear and eye shot. It logs them on the positive or negative side and whatever side weighs more will provide your outlook in life. Attaining success typically takes a while and can be hard work as you learn to fit the pieces together. Having people who add to your negative side makes the journey even harder, like pushing a boulder up a hill, as you then have to counteract their limiting thoughts with even more effort.

Empowering people lift and encourage others. They provide useful strategies to help people reach their goals. They share their contacts and resources with others who align with their thinking and who inhibit the same beliefs as they do. They are risk takers, action takers, and inspire the people around them to reach their full potential.

Become an empowering thinker. Write down your

limiting beliefs and replace them with new empowering beliefs. Take inventory of the negative thoughts you think throughout the day. When a negative thought pops up, make a mental note to stop that thought in its tracks. Realise the thought was negative and immediately replace it with an empowering version of that same thought. Get into a habit of catching negative thoughts before they sink too deep into the mind. This requires you to stay mentally vigilant and on guard towards every thought you think during the day. Soon you will become highly aware of the beliefs you carry that constantly impact the quality of your life.

LET FEAR BE YOUR GUIDE

Doing the things you fear can be scary. You don't know how to react as you are likely unaccustomed to the event at hand. You fumble around, trying to avoid the fear instead of facing it head on and overcoming it. This strengthens the fear and allows it to have more of a grip over you. Instead, do the things you fear. Let fear be your guide.

If you feel fear in certain situations, it means you are weak in that area and need to develop. Once you do, you would elevate mentally, opening up a richer and more interesting experience of the world. It's as if the fear is a wall in front of you that you cannot see beyond. Once you climb over it and get past it, you can see much further.

In the non-life-threatening world we live in today, fear acts as the gateway in becoming the person you want to become. By pursuing your fears you become tougher, more resilient, learn valuable life skills, and can inspire others. Everything you want in life is on the other side of fear.

Say you want to have a loving relationship with your family. You love them deep down, but you are more used to bickering and arguing with them. You're scared to express your feelings with them in case you get shut down or laughed at for being so emotional. You're not sure how they would react, whether reciprocally or uncomfortably. Your fear of the unknown is stopping you from expressing yourself. You know that all you need to do is pull a family member aside and tell them something you appreciate about them, and perhaps share with them that you do in fact love them. The only way through is through! They say, "When you're going through hell, don't stop!". By doing so you would unburden yourself, you would strengthen your mind, and you would take a step closer to becoming the person you want to become.

Get comfortable being uncomfortable. Short-term pain, in the form of embarrassment, is almost guaranteed as you attempt to overcome your fears, but remember you're playing the long game for future gains. The person you are becoming is the reward here. The material 'things' that act as real-life tangible markers, are secondary to the feeling you have of who you feel yourself transforming into.

Let fear wake you up. Every time you feel fear, flick the switch inside your mind to convince yourself you are excited to confront the fear. A physical bodily cue can be exercised when you feel this so you lock in a specific movement to gain access to your fearless state. More on this in the 'Changing Your State' chapter later in this section.

Developing a deeper desire for your goals in life is key to help you break through your fears. When the desire is bigger than the fear, the fear gets steamrolled as you work towards your goals. If you don't have such goals, create some now. Create solid goals that are inevitable to reach if you really committed to them. As you accomplish goals, create new goals to reach bigger and better milestones. By doing so you push your boundaries and become more confident in your abilities. Don't limit your goals to just one area. Think about financial goals, fitness goals, relationship goals, expression goals, rejection goals, and any other goals you can think of.

If you play it safe, you are also numbing your ambition. Over time you can condition yourself to keep your goals too close to you, so you never fail, but also never truly succeed with a big enough win that can change your future significantly. When you play it safe, you live a dull existence. When you go for things involving risk, the rewards are greater and more satisfying. Think about the last time you met someone you took a liking to. You saw them, went over, introduced yourself and put yourself out on the line to be rejected or welcomed. For some, it played out well, you got their info or went on a date. For others, it didn't go so well, you go home disappointed and embarrassed. But if that was the case, you wouldn't go home with regret. You would at least be proud of yourself for acting in the face of fear and giving it your best shot in that moment. The embarrassment highlighted that your skills in that area are not as good as you'd like them to be. Now you are more aware and can learn skills through further practise and experimenting. You find things that work and things that don't work, you learn more about yourself, and the next time you talk to a potential partner, you are more able to handle the situation.

Remember: danger is real but fear is a choice. Use this piece of information to determine whether you would get physically hurt out of the event at hand, or if it is just a fear-inducing event. If it would cause physical harm to you, it's likely a good fear to have and avoid. But if it is something more emotional or mental, then it's just likely to hurt your ego. When you face your fears, there is no regret. You can only win out of it. You either succeed or end up having a learning experience by which you develop. Fear should not be avoided, it should be sought after and experimented with, as with every time you face fear, you learn something that can help you improve your capabilities.

CONDITIONING: BUILDING REFERENCE EXPERIENCES

A friend of mine grew up in a children's home in the 1970s. He described it as a very emotional experience, from being moved around from home to home, to being unsure of his safety when he was victim to the bigger children's bullying. Despite it being tough whilst he was going through it, his experience there massively impacted his overall attitude towards future fear-inducing events. For him, being conditioned with a tougher life from earlier on made other fearful situations seem insignificant in comparison. He had built reference experiences that he could recall in other fearful times, reassuring him that if he got through 'that', he could easily get through 'this'. Fortunately for my friend, he now lives a very happy and content life. However unfortunately for some others, this same experience could lead to lifelong trauma.

You get conditioned from the moment you get pushed out into the world. You get conditioned with your name, with the food you eat, with the clothes you wear, with the environment you get put into, with the people around you and with the experiences you live out. Despite our best efforts to control our influences, we are still susceptible to the subtlest of stimulus.

When it comes to reprogramming ourselves to take on challenges and become the ideal person we long to be, the process, for some, can take a while because of previous conditioning. Using the 'weighing scales analogy', we can see how our behaviour is conditioned by the thinking and actions we have repeated the most over time. Fortunately for us, just one powerful experience is enough to put us on the path towards offsetting a lifetime of limiting and negative experiences.

By building up your reference experiences, you purposefully create new empowering memories that your brain can call on whenever you run into challenging situations. You condition your mind to know you will be okay in any situation you find yourself in. In my earlier example with the girl in the gym, I was terrified. I was scared of public embarrassment, of having to change gyms, of her reporting me to the gym staff for hassling her, for being beaten up by her two beefcake friends if I made her feel uncomfortable. But I wanted to talk to her, I wanted to see what would happen, I had hope, I was scared, but I was still aware enough to realise I was being irrational, so I went for it. I went in and came out unscathed. I pushed a mental boundary. I stepped into my fear and I'm thankful I did.

From that day a mental shift took place and a significant memory was logged in my mind. I realised I could speak to whoever I wanted, I could face fear, become bolder, learn more about myself, and become better at interacting with others. That experience was one that changed me forever, and despite bombing in unspectacular fashion, I will never regret that moment. It allowed me to realise there was more out there waiting for me in the world. I just had to go and get it.

Other than the pretty girl in the gym situation, there have been plenty more experiences where facing my fears proved to bring me great returns. Each time I needed to speak in public, whether in school, when introducing myself to crowds, and when networking for businesses, the fear of public speaking and speaking to audiences was something that made me want to run and hide. When speaking to someone directly, I felt unworthy. As if I would have nothing to contribute to the conversation. In my mind, the people around me were better than me.

They were more able to function together, and I was the one who felt uncomfortable just being there. It wasn't until later in life that I realised many other people have this same experience, and that speaking to people was a skill that could be practised and developed.

In the beginning of my business career, I was expected to speak at events to share what I did and to do my best to educate the crowd. Several days before the event, my mind would race, and I would get anxious when thinking about the speaking engagement. I would practise in my head and hope there were no questions at the end. When the day came, I felt sick. I felt hot and flushed, my blood gushing around my body and bringing me into a state of panic. All I wanted to do was get it over with as soon as possible and even thought about ways I could get out of delivering the speech entirely. But this would have been detrimental to my business's growth and also for my integrity.

I knew I could do better, and I looked in awe at those who skillfully and effortlessly held the crowd's attention when they spoke. On one of my first speeches, with around 30 people in the room, I gave the talk and rushed the entire thing. People didn't know who I was, what I sold, or what I did. I didn't transfer belief in the great product I had to offer. I didn't let them learn anything about me. In my mind it was all about my performance, rather than educating and serving the audience. It was a nerve-racking experience.

Later, after the speaking segment was over, one of the people in the room came up to me and told me I was speaking way too fast. He advised me to slow it down and to share only the parts of the business that were of importance to the people I was speaking to. This made total sense. I initially planned to go over my entire business plan. I was inexperienced and had no references to go by. I was going in blind.

In my mind I failed miserably that day, however in the long run I picked up valuable lessons that I could implement into future speeches that have lasted with me until today. The more I spoke at events, the more I conditioned myself to overcome my fear. I was able to confront it regularly as I had events to speak at each week. I was often in the vicinity of my fear. This allowed me to replace the feeling of fear with feelings of familiarity. I was conditioning myself to get to know what it was like to speak to crowds. It also allowed me to witness other speakers and see their human side, discovering that they make mistakes too and that it was all part of the process. It allowed me to learn about myself and how to deliver more captivating and memorable speeches. The more I did it, the better I became, and the fear seemed to evaporate. Now I look forward to doing speeches. I choose to be excited rather than feel fear. My focus is on best serving the audience and sharing valuable content with them, rather than thinking about how I'm being perceived the whole time.

Conditioning yourself to go after your fears increases your levels of happiness and contentment. You gain control over your mind and you go to sleep knowing you gave it all you had. Choosing not to face your fears strengthens them and allows them to tighten their grip on you even more. Only facing your fears will diminish them. The longer you wait, the more scared you become. The quicker you act on your fears, the more confident you become towards crushing them. Fear is a habit, and the only way to change it is to replace it with a more empowering habit.

By conditioning yourself to act whenever you feel fear,

you gain mastery over your emotions and force your irrational fears to breakdown. Constantly condition and strengthen your mind, so that whatever the world chucks at you, you know deep down, thanks to a reservoir of affirming reference experiences, you have the capabilities and internal resilience to go through the pain period and reach your desired outcome.

"I fear not the man who has practised 10,000 kicks once, but I fear the man who has practised one kick 10,000 times"
— Bruce Lee

CHANGING YOUR IDENTITY: WHO DO YOU THINK YOU ARE?

Once you experience a 'this is enough' moment, or you condition yourself to change by facing your fears progressively, your character will forever be changed. When you overcome fears, you can change your entire identity as you realise you have just been playing a character that has been shaped by your life experiences. When you acknowledge this, you gain the power and responsibility for influencing yourself.

Your ego is the collection of your past experiences that form your sense of self and identity. As a new identity shifting strategy, make 'making the first move' a new character defining trait in you. Imagine yourself as a person who initiates things and gets things moving. Be first to share ideas, develop your wit so you become known for being sharp, offer your help to those who would be grateful, and become known for being a person of action. Make a habit of taking action. By doing so you condition yourself with new reference experiences that back up your new identity.

Visualise yourself as your 'ideal self'. What would you wear? How would you talk? How would you be seen by others? How would you be seen by yourself? Write down all the attributes you want your new identity to have. Vividly imagine what it would be like to inherit these ideal attributes immediately. Embody them and enjoy how they make you feel. Then in the real world, carry yourself and live exactly how you imagined yourself to be.

You teach others how to treat you by the level of respect you hold for yourself. If someone belittles you and you let them get away with it, you subconsciously tell yourself you are not worthy, and you teach that person to continue to treat you in such a way. By being totally observant when in confronting situations, you take away all emotions behind your words. You can ask very direct questions and can point out a person's demeaning behaviour in a relaxed and impactful way. By not lowering yourself to their belittling standards, or inflating your ego to feel superior, your words come from a more aware and mindful source. If they persist, you can cut contact with them until they learn to treat you how you want to be treated.

As mentioned earlier in this book, life is black and white. The grey area is when emotion gets involved. Usually our gut knows what is right and wrong, and we should listen to it. Command nothing less than morally right behaviour, and that is what you will receive.

As each day passes, work at forgetting your past identity and establishing a new, more empowering identity. One that will help you be who you want to be, feel how you want to feel, and live how you want to live. You are the only one who has control over your mind. By taking responsibility for building your new identity, you steer your life in the direction you wish to go.

UPGRADE YOUR FEARS: EMPOWERING FEARS

What's worse: being afraid to confront a fear? Or living with sickening regret from not taking action when you had the chance?

A powerful technique to overcome your fear is by replacing it with a superior, more empowering fear. By using this technique, you employ fear to work for you rather than against you. Let's use the fear of rejection. You have an idea you think would greatly benefit many people's lives, but you fear what the reaction would be from the people you tell this new idea to. On the limiting fear side, you would shy away when it comes time to deliver the passion, belief, and reasoning necessary to sway the crowd. You'd fail to convey your idea's value and look incapable of being the right person for the job.

However, on the empowering fear side, you could instead have a fear like, "I am more afraid of not sharing this idea with people, as if I don't, I would never receive the feedback that would help hone this idea into something even more valuable, and have more of an impact with the people it reaches."

In this simple case, you can see how an easy shift in thinking can empower a person to take action rather than be stifled by negative thinking. Paralysis by analysis is defeated, and action takes the win!

Imagine you're terrified of deep water, but when you weren't looking, your daughter swam far out into a lake. You know she can swim, but after a while her arms and legs begin to tire. You see her struggling and bobbing up and down in the water, gasping for air, almost becoming fully submerged. Your fear of deep water would fly out of the window, and you would race to save your child. There would be no question of fearing water. The fear of something terrible happening to your child would trump any fear you previously held in your mind. Your fear of your child's wellbeing would force you into action. It pushed all minor fears aside, driving you to break your limiting fears and act with an unbreakable level of confidence, doing whatever it takes to keep your child alive. Use this visual example as a reminder that you have the power to overcome your fears if you have a better fear pushing you to fight, rather than to take flight or freeze.

To choose an empowering fear over a crippling fear, you must recognise the greater purpose behind the situation. The question should not be, how do I overcome my fears? Forget about how you overcome your fears. Think about what would happen if you don't overcome your fears? What would happen to your life? How will being fearful destroy your creativity and freedom? What good can come from negative thinking fears? How would you be seen by others if you let fears control you? How would you feel about yourself knowing you let irrational fears rob you of your life?

Empowering fears elevate your thinking and take you to a place outside of your current situation. It gives you a 360-degree, 10,000 feet view. It allows you to take stock of the situation so you can choose the best possible route for the best possible outcome.

Some general empowering fears could be:
> I'm afraid of not being a role model to my children. I'm afraid my children will pick up my limited thinking and think they can't do the things they really want to do in life.
> Building a personal business may be difficult, but I'm more afraid of having someone else

controlling my life and dictating where I should be and what I should be doing.

➢ I'm terrified of not getting a grip on my health and eating myself into an early grave.

➢ I'm afraid that if I don't communicate with my family, the gap between us will continue to increase and it will become harder to have a close loving relationship with them.

➢ I am afraid of the pathetic person I will become, if I continue to come up with excuses of why I can't take action.

➢ I fear not taking chances and having to lie on my deathbed knowing I wasted the one life I had.

Come up with a list of empowering fears that you can relate to different areas of your own life. And when you are in a fearful situation, ask yourself: "What fear can I use to best serve me here?"

THE IS ONLY "NOW"

There is great power in living your life with a high degree of mental presence. Presence is also defined as simply 'being'. It's the ability to be so attentive to what is happening in the very moment you are living in. Whilst in this state of 'presence', you have completely detached from all thinking, and are just witnessing everything that is occurring. You give no judgement or opinions to anything being witnessed. It is merely accepted and acknowledged.

This 'present' state is the same state a blade of grass experiences. A blade of grass does not have thoughts. A blade of grass does not get angry at the wind for blowing too hard. It does not curse the rain for flooding its home. It does not feel joy when the sun shines down on it. It does not wish to be grown in a more nutrient dense field. The blade of grass is present. It simply accepts what is. It accepts the wind, the rain, the sun, and the field. It only experiences this state from its beginning to its end. This blade of grass can be trampled on by a fox, eaten by a dairy cow, or sliced by a lawnmower, and in any case, it will still be as eternally present as it has always been. The blade of grass has no mind to identify with. It has no ego. It has no memories. It has no aspirations. The blade of grass will simply just 'be'.

As humans, our egos get mistaken as our sense of self. Our ego is our personal collection of past thoughts and experiences up till now. We mistakenly link our ego to our identity and think nothing of it. It seems normal, as it's what everyone else seems to do as well. But this mistake often leads us to live our lives through our egos. When we go through a situation, our ego comes with us and we see the situation through the eyes of our ego, rather than how it actually is.

An example of this is when watching a game of football. When we're attached to our ego, we get emotionally charged and root for the team we support, whilst having negative feelings for the opposing team. When our team wins, we are over the moon! When our team loses, we are devastated! Our egos can gain so much emotional charge towards our teams. This could come from the conditioning of enthusiastic family members, our first memories, positive reinforcements when something good happened to our teams, and countless other reasonings. Whereas if we had no ego, we would see a round object travelling through the air, being passed to people, and being struck in the direction of a net held up by white poles.

Our egos give meaning to the things we experience. Most humans celebrate birthdays, but what is a birthday? A year was defined by a human for when the earth had completed one revolution of the sun. But prior to a human figuring this out, were there any birthdays? How could there be? A birthday is a man-made mental construction that holds no truth or significance. It's only because almost every other human on the planet celebrates birthdays that we celebrate ours as well. A tiger in the jungles of India does not understand a birthday. It only knows what is around it in the jungle. It hunts, eats, sleeps, mates, and repeats.

The same goes with a house cat. Organising a birthday party for a cat provides it with no significance. It doesn't know why you give it an extra portion of treats every 365 days, and why you dress it up with a bow tie and party hat. It gobbles up the treat with no thought of why it received a larger portion than normal. And immediately tries to knock off the stupid costume you forced it to wear. It is our egos that timestamp events, so we can relive them for our own self-interested emotional reasons.

I'm not trying to make you depressed here, or make you spend all day meditating as you stare at the wall. I'm just highlighting the fact that we make up a lot of the things we get emotional about. Whether it be birthdays, sporting matches, or many other events that make us enthused or depressed. The point is, we choose! We make all of it up inside our minds! It also means we have the power and control to immediately stop thinking in ways that hurt us and choose to live in ways that help us.

All of your thoughts, every single one, is either future-based or past-based. A thought about the present moment is not possible, as you would have to be without a single thought to become present. A thought is always based in the world of time, not of reality. The thought may be milliseconds apart from when the event being thought about is lived out, but until it actually happens, the thought remains a piece of imagination. Think about a delicious, warm slice of chocolate cake sitting right in front of you. Just that last sentence alone is powerful enough to make you salivate as you read this. Your enjoyment of that slice of cake has started now, and it is all imagination-based. You haven't actually eaten the cake yet, but you can get excited and look forward to doing so. Then you pick up the fork and put the cake in your mouth. It's only at this point, the true enjoyment of the cake can be experienced. Until then, it was all in your mind and imagined.

Now, to bring it back to how this can help you overcome fear. Imagine you are walking through a wooded area that you know has been reported to have a large population of wolves. Many people have entered this section of the woods, but none have returned, apart from news channels sharing images of human bones stripped of flesh. The mere knowledge you are in this environment would put you into a fearful state. You think of every worst-case scenario. Your mind races. All your senses heighten as you try to get out of the woods. You hear everything. The crack of a loose branch breaking as it hits the ground is enough for you to imagine it is the alpha wolf stalking you until the rest of the pack are ready to take you down and rip your throat out of your neck.

The fact is, until you see, feel, or hear the pack of wolves getting closer to you, everything you feel is imagined. It is your mind trying to find patterns where there is none. Your mind runs wild and diverts all your energy into looking out for wolves.

Fortunately, you get out of the woods alive, and scramble over to your car, instantly locking the doors after jumping inside. You're safe, and you are the only person to come out of there unharmed. You vow to never go into that area ever again in your life, even though nothing happened to you, and everything you were experiencing was in your mind. Later, you explain the situation to your friends at the bar, showing them exactly where you were on Google Maps. To your surprise, they inform you the area you were in was actually a nature reserve, dedicated exclusively to the growth and repopulation of the fluffy bunny and beautiful butterfly colonies. You realise the place you thought of had the same name but was located in a different state. The story ends with your friends taking the piss out of you for the rest of time, and every year they hire a magician to turn up at your front door to pull a bunny out of a hat.

You have the power to concentrate your thoughts to experience the truth in every moment. It is a constant practise, as your thoughts will always try to share their voice to influence you, but you have the final say, whether to listen to them or to live in the moment. Fear cannot live in the present moment. It can only live in a thought as an imagined response. You can train yourself to live in the present and to see things as they are, rather than how they have been perceived to be in the mind. By doing so, you can completely eliminate all fears. By silencing the thoughts in the mind, you're rewarded with the appreciation of the moment you are in and can then choose the best path of action that would benefit you most. By taking your ego out of the situation, you can react rationally and have complete control over yourself.

ACTION CURES ALL

It all comes down to action. Action is the cure for everything you wish to gain in life. There are two results that can come out of taking action, either you succeed in the task at hand or you learn something that can help you succeed later on down the line. It's that simple. Action inspires further action. The more you act, the more inspired and motivated you become. Action creates confidence. Action adds to reference experiences. Action changes a person's identity forever. Despite how scary it can be, action will always be your best and most rewarding friend.

Inaction creates doubt. Inaction fertilises fear. Inaction causes events to happen to you, rather than having you influence the event. The longer you do not act, the more the fear builds up and cripples your rational thinking.

Action is vital for you to overcome your fears and to succeed in your endeavours. The quicker you get into the habit of taking action towards your fears, the quicker you can conquer your fears. Make a habit of taking action whenever you feel fear. As soon as you feel fear, start a 10 second countdown and take action before the countdown reaches zero. In the 10 seconds, feel the fear as much as you like. Let it cripple you, let it take control of your body, but by zero, act! No matter what happens to you in the 10 seconds of thinking, do not pass zero without moving to act in some way. The action could be small, or it could be significant, but just make sure you take some real physical form of action. By doing so, you condition yourself to respond whenever fear arises. Eventually, your identity will follow suit, and you will increasingly think of yourself as an action taker, further solidifying the new habit you would have created.

By taking any form of action, you step into the fear and realise it has no hold on you. Any hold it had was purely mental and not tangible. Your higher consciousness then understands it was imagined, and by realising you are still alive and unharmed, your fear disintegrates. Focus on only taking the very next step. Thinking too far ahead is a recipe for overwhelm. By focusing on the next task you can execute on, you eliminate all feelings of overwhelm and fear that come from taking on a mammoth mission.

Remind yourself that pain is temporary, but regret is forever. No one ever regrets doing the things they fear. So many lives have been wasted because of minds controlled by fear. Create a new attitude to fear. Think about the pain you would feel by confronting a fear, compared to the pain you would feel by knowing you missed opportunities and let fear control you. Life is meant to be lived, moments are meant to be seized, expression should be free to flow, and happiness should be practised daily.

Fear is temporary, but not learning from fear can make us live repetitive lives. This stops us from advancing in life and leads us to living lives of quiet desperation and stagnation. Take control of your life by acting in the moment. Force yourself to take action, to build reference experiences, to become familiar with fear, and to create a habit of facing your fears rather than fleeing from them.

CONTROL THE CONTROLLABLE

There are few things you have complete control over in life. You can't decide when you're born, what day your kids will be born, what someone thinks of you, what day you find your ideal partner, or what day you die. So many of the big moments in our life are outside of our control. Anxiety and other stress-related feelings in the body can be attributed to a perceived lack of control. To feel secure, we need to know we are in control of specific things related to our safety. However, when we extend our need for control beyond the essential areas of our lives, we can get met with an opposing force. We can only control the things we have direct access to. This is our own thoughts, words, and actions.

You are only responsible for yourself. You can only control how you think, how you act, how you react, and what you decide to let in or cut out of your life. Having an objective state of mind is powerful as your emotions are set aside, and you see things as they are.

In situations that cause feelings of fear, you can only react to events moment by moment. With situations outside of your control, use the 'ask, attempt, and acknowledge' technique to systematically confront fear. 'Ask' yourself what you are fearing and why you are fearing it. Next, make a strong committed 'attempt' to get through your fear. If you make it through, great, if you don't, it's likely you need to change your approach. Finally, 'acknowledge' the task you are attempting may take time or may need rethinking. If you're patient and determined enough, there's always a way through your fears.

Do the best you can do in any situation you are in by executing one step at a time. Don't think too far ahead as it's impossible to know the exact outcome. Pondering on it at length causes anxiety about the situation as it can be so unpredictable and outside your control. Control only what you can control, which is the thoughts, words, and actions of yourself. Nothing more.

KNOW YOUR WORTH

Fear thrives off insecurities. High self-esteem is a killer of fear. A person with high self-esteem knows they provide value to the people they are sharing their thoughts, ideas, and actions with. It starts with believing in this baseline truth that is true for every single human living today: "Being born means you were the fortunate one out of billions to be chosen to exist. Think about how many millions of years of evolution has had to happen to create you! Every single member of your genetic gene pool has worked hard to stay alive and adapt to allow their offspring to survive. Now it is your time. You are the most important being in your ancestor's legacy. Soon that legacy will be of your creation, so now it's your responsibility to help it succeed and continue surviving."

So how do you build self-esteem? Well, there are many specific techniques, but the overall way to build and create a new lifestyle with a winning mindset is by conditioning yourself into a new identity. Your day-to-day actions must reflect the long-term lifestyle you wish to live.

So, if you are out of shape, get into shape. If you often feel tired and sluggish, eat a healthier diet. If you are not happy with your job, find a new job, or find and work on something you enjoy that can eventually support your lifestyle. If you have money problems, research ways how you can save money where it's possible to save money and find ways to make more money by providing value to others, whether inside your current job, or on your own projects outside of your job. If you have no hobbies, try new things and find something you enjoy. If you can't stop your mind from thinking, learn to meditate starting with one minute a day, and if you feel you can do more, gradually extend the time. If you lack friends, go out to different events to meet and connect with like-minded people. If you have addictions, replace the time you spend partaking in each addiction with healthier addictions that improve the quality of your life. If you think your life is worthless, give some of your time to help someone in a worse situation than you. If your family relationships are not loving, learn how to give love to each member of your family, how they want to be loved, not how you think they should be loved. If you're self-obsessed, practise giving yourself to others and helping them to feel better about themselves where you can, in a non-financial way. If you're easily taken advantage of, practise saying "No" to people when you don't want to go places, do things, or spend time or money.

You see, people treat you how you teach them to treat you. So, respect yourself! Imagine someone is speaking disrespectfully to you. If you don't air your thoughts about their words or actions then and there, you are not living truly to yourself. You must bring up the issue at hand directly but calmly. If you share your ambitions with someone and they belittle you, you need to respectfully inform them that you dislike what they're saying and tell them to stop that behaviour. If people attempt to take advantage of your good nature and guilt you into giving money or time to something you don't want to be a part of, you must exercise your freedom to deny such requests. People will treat you how you teach them to treat you. You condition them by conditioning yourself. If they request unreasonable requests and you continue to deny them, they will soon stop asking you. You will condition yourself to not be someone who gets taken advantage of. You will look internally for your sense of worth, rather than only feeling good when someone else gives you validation.

Trust your gut. Continuously condition yourself with what feels right. Your morals and ethics are the governing factor in what you decide to do and not do. Your morals and ethics know that robbing someone on the street for their money is wrong. It may leave them in a dire situation and could be the difference between life and death for some people. Your morals and ethics also know that creating a business that serves people and asks them to pay a fair price for the product or service is an acceptable, well-intentioned and ethical way to support yourself. By relying on your intuition, you live to your truest self. You do what feels right in the moment, and that cannot give you feelings of regret, as it is your truest intentions expressing themselves. If things go well, you have your intuition to thank. If things go bad, at least you tried, failed, and hopefully learned something out of it. This is better than being burdened with knowing you didn't do what you felt would have been the right thing to do in the moment.

When representing a product or service, you must know it is worthy for your customers and that it will benefit them greatly. Your level of belief in your capabilities to serve the customer, and in your products value to the customer, must be high to convey that their time and money will be well spent. When you have this level of conviction in what you do there is no reason to fear presenting or closing a customer as you have their best interest at heart and know what you have to offer will benefit them. If you don't have this level of conviction, it is likely you're representing the wrong product or service, or you think it needs more work before it is exceptional. It also may be due to your thoughts about selling and your general attitude in life. In either case, work on yourself and the offering until it's something you have total belief in, so you know what you have to offer will undoubtedly improve the customers life.

The same can be said for romantic relationships. When you have total belief in yourself, when you know that by sharing a life or an experience with you, the other person's life would only be positively impacted, there is no room for fear to exist. Your level of conviction in yourself would be so high that all mental roadblocks and doubts would be flattened. The fear of approaching them, of asking them out, of going in for the kiss, or of asking them to marry you would be so insignificant and virtually nonexistent. This is why it's useful to develop your self-worth, as your beliefs about yourself act as an internal compass, guiding you through life, making it a fearful and miserable ride, or an exciting and thrilling journey.

CHANGING YOUR STATE

The fastest way to change your mental state is to change your physical state. Your emotions are naturally connected to your physical positioning. Think about dropping onto a comfortable armchair and slouching down for a couple of hours. Eventually, if not immediately, you can feel relaxed, lazy, tired, unmotivated, and even depressed. Now think about being at your favourite musician's concert, and dancing like no one is watching. Your hands reach for the sky, you're jumping up and down, and singing at the top of your lungs, totally free and uninhibited. Just thinking about either experience can put us into that mental state.

But you don't have to wait until you are in an environment where everyone is partying to feel alive and exhilarated. You can feel that feeling anytime you want, by directing your body in ways to elicit those emotions. Begin by breathing deeply. When you are free and expressive, perhaps when you are laughing or in a joyous situation, how is your breathing? You'll likely fill your lungs deeply with air, and your breathing rate would be slow and relaxed. How about when you are stressed and anxious? It's likely your breathing would then be shorter and sharper, breathing in a restricted way and not performing deep inhalations. Your breath is the simplest and most direct way to changing your state. Practise deep breathing in fearful times. Let it calm you and bring out your confidence. Consciously use it to interrupt and take control of your body's reactions.

Similarly, changing your facial expressions when you experience fear is another great way to change your emotional state. When you are worried and anxious, your face tenses, your forehead wrinkles, and your eyebrows get closer and lift upwards. To change your emotional state, firstly, acknowledge your face is reacting in this way, and secondly, change your face to a more positive reaction, like raising your eyebrows and showing a mouth wide open teeth-baring smile. As you change your facial expression, notice the change in your attitude and the feeling inside you. You may notice you take in a deep breath as you smile, and your body may feel lighter and looser. The more you consciously practise this, the more automatic it will be to change to a state that allows you to remain calm and in control of your reactions.

A 'pattern interrupt' is the name for the ability to catch yourself before you repeat a habitual action. You 'interrupt' the automatic and unconscious 'pattern' and become aware enough to purposefully implement a new habit or action.

When you experience an irrational fear and your body tenses up, or you experience a negative feeling inside your body that you dislike, for a few seconds, deliberately shake your body, arms, legs, and head, as if you are an athlete loosening up for the 100 metre sprint. This intentional pattern interrupting action forces you to become present and gives you immediate control over your physical and mental states. You create a mental gap between you and the negative physical and emotional state. This gap is enough to bring clarity to the task at hand. It expands your perspective and it allows you to choose the best path to get you through the challenge and closer to your goal.

Next, create your own physical ritual you can use in situations where you need to gain immediate control over your reactions and emotions. A ritual I often use to get into an action taking state is to hit my fist on my chest 3 times. A mental switch takes place in my mind and I feel transformed into my most free, confident, and expressive self. Whilst doing so I would intentionally smile, opening my eyes and mouth wide, and take in a deep breath. By performing this conditioned action, I can't help but enter the state required for me to get through the challenging situation. Whether it ended in a success or a failure, the point of it is I took action, and I could live true to myself and free of regret.

Along with a physical gesture, having a phrase can also act as a trigger to get you to act through fear. In relation to the story at the beginning of this book, with the pretty girl in the gym, the phrase "Fuck it, I'll do it" became a trigger for me to overcome the fear in front of me in the moment. Create a powerful phrase for yourself that you can call on in moments when fear is near. Having explosive, energy rich movements and phrases is great to condition you to get used to breaking the fear barrier.

These work well when alone, but when in crowded places or when in the middle of a fear-inducing situation, it may be a bit over the top. In these situations, a smaller, less expressive version of the same gesture and phrases can work just as well. If in the heat of a fearful moment, I want to get myself into a state of confidence and full expression, casually tapping my fist on my chest 3 times, as if something you would do when trying to get rid of some gas, whilst smiling softly and inhaling deeply, is enough to get me into a peak state and ready to take on any challenge. Experiment with and adopt your own physical gestures and phrases that would help you get to your peak state when you need it.

As mentioned in an earlier chapter, another pattern interrupting technique you can use to break your fear is to act on them within 10 seconds. As soon as you feel fear towards something, count backwards from ten to zero, and by the time you get to zero, start an action that will take you into and through that fear. Over time, the more you practise this technique, the quicker you will act on your fears, and the time can be shortened down to 3 seconds. The trick is to never let yourself go past zero. Change the word 'zero' to something powerful like 3, 2, 1 . . . Execute! Or 3, 2, 1 . . . Let's go! Condition yourself to act with a countdown combined with a physical state change. Whilst counting down, use your physical pattern interrupt to mentally pump yourself up, making you excited to take action. Then by the time you hit zero, take action! And as an added benefit of this process, you add another positive reference experience for your mind to use in future situations.

As a failsafe to this technique, another physical pattern interrupt can be implemented by wearing a rubber band on your wrist. Keep a rubber band on your wrist, and if you fail to act within the 10 second countdown, or after the physical gesturing and power-phrase state change, pull hard on the rubber band and let it slap back into you. This technique uses physical pain to condition you to fear the pain of the rubber band more than fearing the pain of going through the fear. This technique works as we are motivated to avoid pain and seek pleasure. Knowing we would experience pain if we didn't execute on our fears is enough to force us into action. (By the way, don't be a pussy about it, really go for it. Pull the fuck out of that rubber band. The greater the pain, the more we will be motivated to act to avoid it.)

Another great way to get out of your head and into a better state is through self-amusement. Self-amusement is a private joke between you and yourself. The idea is to make yourself laugh by purposefully doing something silly to make fun out of yourself and your ego. The trick is, it needs to be something you genuinely find funny. Its effect is it helps to loosen you up. It frees you from having to hold yourself up to a perfect vision of yourself and it gives you permission to be fun, light-hearted, and human. Laughter always provides good feelings in the body. It relaxes you and makes you feel free. It is impossible to feel fear when your body is expressing fun, joy, and happiness.

There isn't really a cookie cutter example for self-amusement as everyone's idea of humour differs, but something like asking someone directions to where the nearest pharmacy is, when you're literally standing right outside of it can't help to bring out a laugh, as the person questions your sanity and seriousness of the question. You laugh, they laugh, everyone's a winner, but you get the added bonus of loosening up, and it gives you permission to push your boundaries when you're in this 'lighter' state.

RESILIENCE AND RESOLVE

"Whether you think you can, or think you can't, you're right"
— Henry Ford

The fear of looking silly plays a big part in why many people don't attempt their bigger goals or ambitions in life. The expected feeling of vulnerability they would experience stops them from freely putting out their thoughts, ideas, or products. It's impossible to know the enormous number of great ideas that could have drastically impacted the world, but never saw the light of day. A number of them could be down to genuine reasons, where a person did everything they could, but the ideas just didn't take off. But many ideas could have never been attempted because the people who thought them cared more about how they were perceived in the world and didn't want to be seen failing. This is sad and heartbreaking. The amount of people that fear what others will say about them if they fail makes them not even attempt to begin with. Some live the rest of their lives knowing they never tried to be as great as they could have been. Some turn into the cynical, judgemental people whose opinion they were so afraid of. But making mistakes is all part of the process.

The truth is, once you become so set on a goal, and know you will do whatever it takes for it to be reached, nothing has the power to stop you. You learn what you need to learn, you connect with who you need to connect with, and you do what you need to do to get to your desired outcome. Developing belief in yourself, and in your ability to learn and apply, is the difference between those who succeed and those who quit or never even try.

By taking the long-term approach, the minor bumps in

the journey may slow you down, but they don't stop you. You embrace the fact that you are bound to make mistakes, but know deep down, you have what it takes and are resourceful enough to eventually turn it around.

It's useful to live with a positive mental attitude towards every area of your life. Actively gain as much knowledge as you can to help you on your purpose. It is possible to find a nugget of information that could advance you in some way from every situation you are in. Adopting this outlook helps you to come across more beneficial situations that you can take advantage of. Thinking miserably never got anyone anywhere and likely makes people want to avoid you. Life is short and taking yourself too seriously will only bring you a life of limited experiences and feeling unfulfilled. Being light and breezy is fun, it is attractive, and people want to spend time with someone who provides feelings of joy and amusement.

Someone who has a positive outlook on life can accept things will not always go their way. They understand success in any endeavour may take longer than first expected, but they have the resolve and foresight to stick it out as the rewards later down the line are worth it.

LIVING WITH INTEGRITY

Regret is poison for the soul. It is a feeling reminding you that in some scenario, you did not act with integrity. It chips away at you, and it doesn't go away until you do what you know you need to do. Regret results from not listening to your gut. Your gut is your internal compass that guides you throughout life, based on your morals, ethics, and values. It is sticking up for what you believe in, it is voicing your opinion, it is executing where you need to execute, it is living with integrity and fully expressing yourself.

Even the smallest regrets can last a lifetime. Taking action or holding back can create a huge difference in the life you live later on down the road. Say a friend offered you a chance to be a partner in their business. You knew it was a good idea, and it all worked out on paper, but you feared what your family would say, as all your evening and weekend time would be spent working on the business until you could quit your day job and have it support your lifestyle. You didn't trust your gut, so you turned down the offer. You walk away, never knowing the possibility of whether the business would be a success. 5 years later, your friend who offered the business to you has created a substantial amount of wealth for himself. You see him a few times a year in person, but on social media you see him every other day enjoying his luxurious lifestyle. You, on the other hand, are stuck in the same job you were in 5 years ago and are not any happier or fulfilled. As life continues, he builds bigger businesses, invests in more projects, creates relationships with other successful people, goes on amazing holidays every month, and secures his and his families future indefinitely. While for the next 30 years, you continue to wake up at the crack of dawn to build someone else's business. You have to ask someone else for permission if you can take a day off, you don't feel appreciated, and you can't wait to get home every day. And as each day rolls by, the regret eats away at your mind.

Imagine every morning when waiting for the train to get to work, you see a really gorgeous girl standing on the same platform as you. I'm talking stunning, a real 10 out of 10. Every day you both board the train and take subtle peeks at each other throughout the journey. You can tell she likes you, and you clearly like her. Could she be a fling? A girlfriend? Perhaps eventually she could be your wife and the mother to your children? Who knows…? It all relies on you to build up the courage to say something to her. To break the ice and ask her out. It's simple really. But your fears get the best of you. You think it's creepy, you think she would be uncomfortable, you think too many people can hear your interaction. You think of so many bullshit reasons not speak to her that you do exactly that. Then, one day, another commuter arrives on the platform and likes the look of her. Unfortunately for you, he goes straight in. He fumbles around, but she likes his confidence and is amused by his unpolished approach. They switch numbers, and over the course of a few weeks you get to witness them getting closer, laughing together, touching, kissing, and doing all of that cute shit. You try to stop looking and convince yourself there's plenty more fish in the sea, which is true, but deep down you know that could have been you, if only you weren't so afraid of making the first move. She's off the market and immediately stops glancing over in your direction. Eventually, they get married and move out of town, so you never see her again, but you're left wondering what could have been.

It works the same way for a girl who likes a guy. I know people who haven't yet learned from their past and continue to make the same mistakes year after year. Next thing they know, their youth is gone, and the time they can afford to have fun with is over.

We could come up with thousands of examples here, but you get the point. Don't let your life be filled with regret by not taking action on the things you know you should do. Express yourself truly, fully, and live with high integrity. The pain of regret far outweighs the pain of discipline. Disciplining your actions allows for freedom later down the line. Your fears are temporary, but your regrets will live with you forever. Don't concern yourself with the opinions of others. Take control of your mind and be more concerned with what you think of yourself. Living for others is the source of unhappiness and anxiety. Living with integrity can only bring about contentment and the freedom of expression we all seek.

HAVING GOALS

Human nature is to set and achieve goals. A baby unconsciously sets a goal to walk once it sees everyone around it walking. A toddler sets a goal to climb on their siblings back to steal cookies out of the cookie jar. A teenager sets a goal to 'get some' by prom night. A university student sets a goal to 'get some' every night, and maybe to pass their final exams if they have time. Someone in their twenties sets a goal to find someone significant in their life before 30. Someone in their thirties sets a goal to have a house, kids, and a stable career. The older we get, the more goals we have set and achieved.

Having direction in life provides you with the creativity needed to achieve something out of your reach. It gives you a reason to push past certain fears and continue executing until you get to the finish line. If you want to make a big difference in the world and influence millions, it's likely you'd need to communicate to large groups of people to present your ideas and plans. You would need to learn and develop leadership skills for others to want to listen to you. You would need to put your reputation on the line and hold yourself accountable. You would need to convince people they can trust you and that you are the right person for the job. By having the end goal in mind, the minor challenges and fears take a back seat as your main driving force is your determination to achieve your vision.

Let's say the vision you have for the romantic side of your life is to meet your ideal partner, get married, buy a house, have kids, cats, dogs, and the white picket fence, but you're afraid to meet new people. You may be a bit of a loner and feel out of your comfort zone when around strangers. You may be bad at communicating, flirting, being intimate, or making people laugh. All the cards may be stacked against you, but if your goal and vision is strong enough, it will drive you through the challenges you need to go through to become the person who deserves such a life.

You would read dating books, you would develop your communication skills, you would push your comfort zones and strike conversations with new people, starting small and building your way up. You would invest in the personal development that would change you into the person you wish to become. You would create so many good behaviours and habits that serve you that meeting new people becomes something you do effortlessly. Eventually, your self-confidence is sky-high, thanks to your newly developed skills, that you look forward to interacting with people wherever you go.

Perhaps you want to own your own business to achieve a level of financial freedom that you won't get by working as an employee, but you fear what others around you will think about you. You fear others will not support you and that your relationships will deteriorate as you spend more time building your vision than hanging out with them. To get around that you could work on your communication skills so you get better at explaining your vision to your friends and family in a way that makes them want to support you. You could network with people who could help you get to your vision. You could learn to develop internal validation and strength, rather than trying to please others. You could realise that people will always talk about you, whether you're doing good or bad, and you could learn to not pay attention to their opinion of you, as at the end of the day, it's you who's responsible for the level of success you attain in life. You would try and fail repeatedly, but eventually you would gain the knowledge, skills, and abilities needed to become financially free and control your life.

By having a solid goal you are committed to achieving, the fears that arise will just as quickly be flattened as you continue on your path towards realising your goal. Goals give you something to live for. They give you a reason to continue learning, developing, and taking action. A good goal embraces the fact that at some point facing fears will be inevitable. If it doesn't, it's likely your fear is limiting you into thinking too small. A good goal gives you hope, a reason to wake up, and makes you feel good about yourself and your future.

Create emotional, powerful goals in several areas of your life and actively take part in achieving them. Don't just be a dreamer, be an action taker! Create a plan of action and execute until the goals are achieved. As fears arise, use the strength of achieving your meaningful goals to force you to face the fears. With practise and familiarity, your fears will lose their strength and have no hold over you.

HUMANISING PEOPLE: TAKING THE P***Y OFF THE PEDESTAL

A lot of the fears we have are in relation to other people. They are more day-to-day social fears rather than life-threatening fears. The fear could be of being left out, of being rejected, of being looked down on, of being disliked, of being banned, mistrusted, and labelled, among many other social fears. The link between them is that they are all fears of what other people think of us.

We all have people who we consider 'higher' than ourselves. This could mean 'higher' financially, or in social status, in influence, in leadership, in fitness, in business, in philanthropy, in romantic relationships (a.k.a punching above your weight), in peer-to-peer relationships, and in family relationships. In fact, we can feel fear towards someone just because they have something we want in some form. We want their ability to influence, or to have their level of wealth, or to be liked and trusted as highly.

We see successful people and we want their results immediately. We forget that the person we perceive them to be took time to develop. They are not superhuman, they are not comic book heroes, they are not above us in any way. They are human! They are just like us, but they have further excelled in an area that we wish to excel in. They may be several steps ahead of us, but their results can be replicated and surpassed if we are committed to getting there.

You could also fear them as they could just be dicks. They could be rude or belligerent, arrogant or obnoxious, or they could just get under your skin. You could fear them because of being in awe of them, or because you're overwhelmed by their wonderful personality. Whether you fear certain people for their positive attributes or their

128

negative attributes, one thing is a fact: they are still just human!

By acknowledging they are just human, it lessens the effect of what they say or do. You take them off the pedestal your mind puts them on and can treat them equally as the humans they are.

If you are in awe of someone and fear speaking to them in case you fumble your words, get tongue tied, or look like an admiring idiot, acknowledging their human side brings them back down to earth for you. Then you can interact with them affectively, putting your best self forward and being better able to seize the opportunity.

They may affect you negatively. You may fear confronting them about issues you disagree with, because perhaps they are better at communicating than you are. Realise the only reason they can 'out speak' you is because they have had more time to hone their debating skills.

They aren't doing anything special. They are human. They wake up with morning breath just like the rest of us, they pick their noses, wipe the gunk out their eyes, piss, fart, and excrete constantly. They could be beautiful and flawless to look at, but underneath their gorgeous skin is the same muscle fibers, bones, and veins in all of us. They breathe the same air we breathe, they drink the same water we drink, they have the same 24 hours a day we have.

Realise you are as capable as the person you fear. If they are a human, then you can match or even surpass them if you worked harder and smarter than they did. Put yourself out there, extend yourself into the things you're afraid of, learn more about the fear, learn skills that will help you advance with them, adapt in the moment rationally and accordingly, have the resolve to make things happen, and be grounded in the reality that you are just like every other human that popped out of the womb. The only difference is the beliefs you have been conditioned to believe, versus the beliefs they have been conditioned to believe.

Remember this fact the next time you're in a situation where you fear something about the person you wish to interact with. Whether it's the CEO of your company who is never seen interacting with anyone outside of the board of directors, the girl you see on the train when you go to work every morning, the Hollywood celebrity, the seemingly untouchable business icon of the century, or anyone else, remember that apart from the different experiences you have been conditioned with, you are both human.

You, just like them, are evolved talking apes, spinning on a ball of water, circling a giant ball of fire in the sky, surrounded by nothingness until you get to the next giant ball of fire billions of miles away. You are small in the grand scheme of things. So is the person you are irrationally fearing. When you change your perspective on how you view humans, you also change the amount of control you allow them to have over you. Take them off the pedestal by increasing your own value to others and your sense of self-worth.

Learn the relevant communication, influence, self-esteem, and presence skills. Condition yourself by interacting with the people you fear in short bursts until you can build enough confidence in yourself and your abilities. Confidence is created through competence. By building up your reference experiences, you become more comfortable with new situations, and as your abilities increase, you are better able to make the most of the moment.

EMBRACE AND EXPERIMENT WITH FEAR

Fear is like an eye floater. You know that little dark patch that appears in your vision when you look up into a bright blue or cloudy white sky. Then when you try to look directly at it, it shifts its position and you never end up getting a good look at it. Well fear has the same qualities. We can feel its presence, we know it is there, but we tend to look past it, or around it, or try to take paths that will avoid us going straight for it. But if we looked right at it and stepped into the fear, we'd see it move away as we get closer to it.

Fear is only present when something is attempting to stop us from doing something. However, by stepping into the fear, we strip it of its potency as we break the mentally imposed barrier that fear urges us not to cross. With each step into the fear, the easier it is to see how fictional it is, and it loses its strength over us.

The next time you feel fear towards something, step into the fear. Experiment with it, see how far you can push it. Play with it, make it fun, like a game between you and yourself. First feel what it feels like when it takes control of your emotions. Then feel how you feel when you take action in the face of your fears. Bathe in the feeling of pushing past your fears. Relish it! Realise if you can do it once, you can continue doing it every time you feel fear. In a very short time, you will look to embrace these fearful moments as it gives you a chance to learn more about yourself and you will know exactly how to overcome the fear. You will end up seeking out fears because of how it makes you feel once you conquer them. You will have the confidence to know everything will work out just fine for you as you have previous experiences to rely on to prove that is the case.

Next time you're in an anxiety filled moment, step into the anxiety and go in with a curious mind. Learn and discover what you're anxious about and how to overcome it. Next time you're about to have a panic attack, for curiosity's sake, step into the state of panic and experience what it is like from a more aware viewpoint. This process requires introspection and a keen attention to detail. Let the feeling wash over you and remain aware of what is happening. Let it completely overcome you and realise you are still standing, you are still alive, and you are still just as you were moments ago. Then, as the fear is at its peak, relish in that feeling. Get comfortable with all the uncomfortableness. Before you know it, the potency of the fear cannot affect you. The fear will melt away and wash right past you. As it does, stay conscious to what is happening in your mind and body. See how you react to every phase of the event and inquisitively learn about what happens to you in the moment.

Stepping into the fear is a powerful technique that allows you to consciously 'dive into the deep end' in an entirely self-controlled way. Like all the techniques mentioned in this section, they best work with continuous and repetitive use. Frequently practise using them all or just the ones that resonated with you the most. Use them to unlock your full potential and master your fears and emotions from now on.

MY BIGGEST FEAR

Out of all the fears discussed in this book and all other fears that haven't been mentioned, my biggest fear is the fear of not living up to my potential. Not living up to your potential messes with your mind. It leaves you with regret, and it forces you to squeeze as much juice out of life as possible. We all have off days when we feel like relaxing and recuperating, so I'm not talking about these times. I'm talking about times when we know we could do something productive but end up wasting it watching shows on television or other pointless pursuits just to fill the time.

This for me is scary. It leaves me feeling uneasy. It becomes a driving factor in my efforts to build, create, and provide value to the world and myself. It helps me sleep better at night as I have the satisfaction of knowing I put everything I had into the day. I have fewer worries on my mind because I know I executed on the things I could control that day. It gives me perspective on the things I spend my time on, establishing whether it is a productive task or just a time-wasting activity. Not living up to my potential has become an immensely empowering fear for me. I can hold it above any feeling of fear, and it will trump it.

Imagine dying and seeing a condensed movie clip of the life you just lived. Then once that's over, you get presented with a movie of the life you could have lived if you just faced up to your fears and lived with high integrity. From my early years till my early twenties I didn't live to my truest self. I held myself back mentally and would paint drastically fearful pictures in my mind that stopped me from doing the things I wanted to do, being with the people I wanted to be with, and living how I wanted to live. Two decades of opportunities missed and wasted! I can never get that time back. It leaves me with a bitter taste of what my life could have been now if I just acted back then. Of course, I didn't have this information to use back then and we all pick up on lessons in our own time, but had I known these skills back then, who knows what my life could have looked like now.

However, from my early twenties onwards I had had enough of being a victim of my fears. I purposefully learned about fear, how it controls people, how to use it for my advantage, how it is not real, how it is all mind manufactured, and how people are left miserable and unfulfilled by cowering to it. Since then I have lived true to my gut. I have done what I wanted to do, expressed myself when I needed to, met the people I needed to meet but were intimidated by, forced myself into situations where it was sink or swim and ended up swimming out of every one of them. I purposely conditioned myself to this way of living, so now my conscience is clear. I am not left with feelings of, 'What if?'. I trained myself to always execute when fear arises, and I live with an unburdened mind. I leave everything I have out on the field. I am fully expressed. I am free.

What **WAS** the biggest fear in your life until now?

....
....
....
....

Why?

....
....
....
....
....
....

NOW, after learning how to use fear, what is the thing you **WANT** to fear the most in your life?

....
....
....
....

Why?

....
....
....
....
....
....

SECTION 3:
DEATH:
THE FINAL ELEMENT

I knew a man called Wesley. We met on an audio-visual installation job we were both working on. He was from South Africa and had moved over to London to earn money and to experience more of the world. He shared a story with me of one of his friends he grew up with, let's call him Sam. Sam was in the construction industry back in South Africa and just started his own family. He had a wife and two kids. To make a living and to support his family, Sam worked over 112 hours a week. That's over 16 hours per day, 7 days a week, rarely allowing him to get in more than 6 hours of sleep each night. After doing that for a couple of years, his body couldn't take the strain it was under and Sam died of a major heart attack. He was 29 years old. His family were devastated, and Wesley then shared with me that that was also a big reason why he left

South Africa. He wanted to get away after the death of his friend. He also didn't want to suffer the same fate Sam had. Wesley decided to move to another country where he didn't know anyone to see what he could make out of himself.

It got me to think and empathise with others, who despite their feelings of fear and hesitancy, take a leap into the unknown to go after the things they desire. Those who start businesses for the sake of their freedom. Those who travel to other ends of the planet to see if life for them and their families will be better for it. Those who go against the people they love and go after their dreams because they know it's the only thing that could make them fulfilled. I respect these people greatly. I came to appreciate the gifts I had been lucky enough to be born with. It also humbled me as I realised, we could all die at any moment, and that I needed to live my life with high integrity, doing what I want, when I wanted to, because I may not get another chance to.

EGOTISTICAL DEATH

It's commonly been said that we are born with only two fears: loud noises and falling. Everything else we pick up along the way. Our egos are the collection of experiences we live out in our lives. It tints how we perceive and interpret things to be. Our egos hold on to everything, and whether or not you realise it, it controls our lives.

When irrationally fearful situations arise, we must learn to kill our egos. All fear is the egos form of death. A fear has a way of playing a self-fulfilling role to the ego. It pumps up the ego, intensifying the fear, and makes us hesitant to do the things we think about doing. The ego and our sense of identity are intertwined, so by killing the ego we are in effect killing off a part of our identity. This is good, as once a limiting part of our identity is destroyed, we gain the clarity and ability to add a fearless and better serving quality to our identity.

To get over any fear, you must kill your ego in relation to that fear. Murder it, over and over again every time it arises. Always choose to be in the 'now', the present moment, instead of being overrun by limiting thoughts. With training and practise you become able to detach yourself from your mind and live more in your body, seeing things as they truly are, rather than how the ego has interpreted things to be. By doing this you see yourself as you truly are, which is eternal presence. Think about when you were a newly born baby. You didn't have any beliefs or thoughts, you were simply in input mode. You absorbed all the information you saw, heard, felt, smelt, and tasted. You didn't have opinions on things because it was all new to you. Everything prior to your ego being developed is your natural state. It is a state of witnessing everything, how things work, what you do, what others do, seeing it all factually without interpreting it as anything other than it actually is.

To get back to this mental position, the secret is to relentlessly kill the idea of the 'self' you identify with every time it resurfaces. By doing this you realise the idea of death is not real. Our egos can die, but the witnessing presence that we really are can never die. It is always there. It is pure consciousness itself. By killing your ego, you strip away all that is not truly you, and you're left as the pure consciousness you really are. The only way for you to be free is to kill your ego in every moment. It will always try to speak out as long as you live. It is a lifelong practise.

LIFE AFTER DEATH

Do you ever get the feeling like no matter what happens to you, you'll be just fine? Almost like you're invincible and can't fathom the essence of death? As if you're going to live forever, in one form or another?

If you do, this is very common. In fact, this never-ending essence is what most religions preach, from Hinduism promoting reincarnation leading to nirvana, and Christianity promoting heaven. Kings and Queens in the ancient Egyptian era believed they could transform their souls into God-like beings through death rituals and mummification. Today, science is developing ways to allow people to live forever by transforming people's consciousness into digital formats, so people can live on as software in a RoboCop-like reality. Okay, to be honest I'm not sure whether I saw that concept in a movie or not, but hey, if it ain't here yet… it's coming!

This feeling of invincibility is linked to who you are at your core, pure consciousness. The reason you feel invincible is because you are. You are eternal presence. Your ego and sense of identity will die, your body will perish, but the consciousness you experience when no thoughts are in your mind will live on forever. It is nothing to identify with, it simply just is.

When we die, we go back to our original state. We become everything and everything becomes us. Death is a human construct. We came from nothing and we'll go to nothing. Nothing is our true existence. We are no thing. When we die, we take another form, a higher form, a more conscious form, consciousness itself. We become everything that was, that is, and that will ever be. We are eternal. We are consciousness.

Some of you may follow me here. To others, it may

seem like I've been lying in the sun for too long before writing that last paragraph, but it is the simplest way to explain who we are at our core. We are all one consciousness experiencing itself subjectively. There is no such thing as death, because we are consciousness itself and consciousness can never die. 'We' as we identify with, are the imaginations of ourselves. The idea of 'we' existing is not tangible. The idea of 'me' is the collection of experiences I have experienced until now. It is an image of myself I have created over time and is not the pure entity I originally came as.

Imagine you lived forever. When I say 'you', I mean your identity, your ego. Imagine you got to live out every fantasy you had, you got to explore every inch of the planet, you got to indulge in every single possibility and explore everything. All your sexual fantasies were met, you became the richest person in the world, you had all the fame in the world, and everyone alive respected you. Sounds great right? And for a while it would be amazing. But eventually, once you do everything that could be done twice, three times, four times, ten times, one hundred times, a thousand times, or ten thousand times, you would be bored out of your skull. You wouldn't be able to fulfil yourself. You would not give any importance to things as you would know you could do it again whenever you wanted to. Your initial euphoria would soon wear off. Luckily for us all, our ego only lasts as long as our physical body does. As far as we know it, physically dying is the end of our ego and identity.

Death gives us urgency. Its inevitability makes us appreciate life and not take things too seriously. If we're lucky, we end up choosing to partake in things that give us the most joy and happiness.

The truth is, everything you do will eventually be

forgotten and destroyed. You are not real. The physical 'you' is real, but the mental 'you' is an imaginary construction. Your personality is not tangible. Your body is. The 'you' you identify with does not exist. Every time you think of your identity, it is a thought that is either past-based or future-based. It thinks of things that either are about to happen or have happened already. The present moment is the only thing that truly exists. It is the very moment we always live in. By acknowledging this moment, it immediately brings you to reality. To stay there, you must relentlessly remain mindful to the moment. Your ego's incessant thoughts will always eventually come back. They relish in occupying your mind and attention. If your thoughts succeed in shifting your focus, you get taken out of reality again. There is only one reality, and that is now. Not in a second from now, not a second ago, but this very millisecond. There is no fear here, as fear is a thought-based mental creation. In the present moment there is only life as it truly is: fearless and free.

DEATHS INEVITABILITY: THE BLUNT REALITIES

"Man surprised me most about humanity. Because he sacrifices his health in order to make money. Then he sacrifices money to recuperate his health. And then he is so anxious about the future that he does not enjoy the present; the result being that he does not live in the present or the future; he lives as if he is never going to die, and then dies having never really lived."
- Dalai Lama

We are all eventually going to die. To live a life worth living, we must not fight this fact. It is far better to go with it, to embrace it. Better still, let it give you hope for the rest of your worldly existence. By realising dying is inevitable and by losing your fear of death, you happily take more worthwhile risks as you know death comes to us all anyway. So why wouldn't you take a risk, when your life will come to an end no matter what you do?

The reality is, death is the end of our identities as we know it. We don't know of a future past it. No one does. The only real ending is death. Death is the only thing you have to do in life. Everything else is a choice with consequences, this is including everything from drinking water to breathing. Death is the only guarantee you get in life, everything else is up for debate.

Your Insignificance

Realise how insignificant you are. When you die, life will go on without you. I urge you to get your 'creep mode' on for one minute every single day. By 'creep mode' I mean this: go to a place in your work, home, or leisurely environment once a day, and for a single minute put yourself in a position where you can see other people, but they cannot see you. From this point, just watch and witness everything that's going on (don't do anything that is actually creepy at this point). Just watch people walking, interacting, keeping busy, and just being themselves. Do this without making yourself seen or heard. When doing so, acknowledge how the world would keep spinning, with or without you. People will still exist, they would not know who you were, and they don't care. You are not as important as your ego thinks you are. Your existence will not change the fact life will go on without you.

What Do You Want?

Some people die without establishing a purpose or calling in life. They work and die, giving no thought to why they are here and what impact they could have on the world. Others who decide on a purpose and live their lives in such a way can contribute more to the world. They can have more, give more, and impact more lives. The question you can ask yourself is: do I merely want to survive life, or do I want to thrive and make the world benefit from my existence?

Either way, you will die. The wind will blow through the trees, waves will continue to crash, your treasured possessions will just lie there and eventually disintegrate back into the earth. Nothing you do or have has any meaning in the grand scheme of things. You are the deciding factor to the level of importance and meaning you feel towards things.

The reality as it is, without beliefs distorting the vision, is that none of it matters. We are all the same. We are all going to die. We are all going to be forgotten. All of our life's work will be destroyed and returned to the earth, which itself, would be smashed or burned into nothing. So, with that in mind, how can you care about the opinion of others? How can you live as inferior to anyone else? We are all not going to be shit.

I'll admit it, I'm purposely going down the negative route here, but you should realise it's also very freeing. It gives you permission to live truly to yourself. It's not a free ticket to go out murdering, raping, and pillaging as much as you want, as you still have your morals to guide you away from negative behaviours. But it does give you a ticket to embrace yourself. To do what you want to do, to be who you want to be, to act how you want to act. None of it matters! Just enjoy yourself while you are alive. You, or anyone else you know, are not that important to existing as a whole. It came from nothing and it will end in nothing. We live alone, we die alone, and everything in between is just an illusion.

• • • • •

To end this chapter, here is an opposite, admittedly less apocalyptic but equally serving perspective for you to consider:

Your Legacy and Humanity

Everything you do is for the greater good of humanity. Everything you do will impact the lives of every person you come into contact with.
Your genetics will go down to all in your legacy.
For every thought you have and every act you do, the impact of how it will affect your future generations should be considered.

• • • • •

Your reality is your decision. How you view the world comes down to you. Let your perspective serve you, not enslave you.

Before going on to the next chapter, take a moment to answer the following questions. Use these questions to bring more awareness to the current mindset of your life.

➢ What do you want to do before you die?
➢ What can you do with your life to make the world a better place?
➢ How would you spend today if you found out you will die tomorrow?
➢ What do you spend too much time doing?
➢ What don't you spend enough time doing?
➢ What new habit do you wish to form?
➢ What is your biggest fear?
➢ How do you see yourself?
➢ What is important in your life?
➢ Why do you do what you do?
➢ How can you take what you learned today, to make your life better tomorrow?
➢ What are you thankful for in this very moment?
➢ What are you curious about lately?
➢ What is the first memory of your life?
➢ Where do you find peace?
➢ What do you miss the most?
➢ What does success mean to you?
➢ What would you do if you had all the money in the world?
➢ What would you do if you had all the time in

the world?

➤ What could you do today that you couldn't do a year ago?

➤ If you knew you had one hour left to live, who would you want to be with for your last hour on this planet?

➤ How do you need to live on a day-to-day basis to die complete?

USING DEATH AS MOTIVATION TO ACT NOW

"Just as a well-filled day brings blessed sleep, so a well-employed life brings a blessed death"
- Leonardo da Vinci

Living an adventurous life, filled with new experiences and venturing into the unknown, will always elicit fear responses within the body. When venturing in unfamiliar territory, you will always feel fear, but what changes is your ability to handle and overcome it. The more you take action when fear strikes, the less affect the fear has on you the next time. Eventually, you become so familiar with the fear it is completely eradicated in that area of your life.

Peace of mind is a quality that should take high priority. When you act with integrity, no doubts can enter your mind. You are doing what you think is the right thing to do in that moment. By living honestly, you rid yourself of having regrets later down the line. You can rest assured knowing you put everything you had into everything you do. In doing so, you leave the situation with a clear mind.

If you're lucky enough to do so, when you look back at your life in your final days, would you be more disappointed with the things you did, or the things you didn't get to do? Would your memory of your life be a list of fears, or a collection of wonderful experiences? If your life ended tomorrow, what would you regret not doing?

I'm terrified of lying on my death bed and thinking, "I know I could have done better". That thought frightens me into action. I scare myself to my core thinking about missed opportunities, relationships, and experiences I could have been a part of. When I reminisce on the things I did in my life, I want to say to myself "Dude, you're a crazy fucker, but you did it". That's what I think life's about, soaking as much of it up as you can, until your time ends, and you clock out.

To live to our fullest self, we must control our minds rather than letting our minds sweep us off our feet. When you are in situations that evoke feelings of boredom, routine, struggle, and fear, remind yourself of your own death. Bring yourself back to reality and see the fragility of your life as it is.

Life is like a video game. You can't get better at playing it by just reading the manual. You have to get stuck in, you have to put in the hours, you have to play! Overcoming your fears is a skill you only develop through experience. The more you partake, the faster the fear evaporates. By not playing the game you may as well be dead. As far as we know it, we only get one life. There are no resets, no extra lives, no respawns. Imagine you just bought a new games console and chucked in your brand-new Grand Theft Auto CD. It starts in the house you'll be living in. Imagine you then potter around the house, shuffling from one room to the next, doing absolutely fuck all in the process. Fuck that! You want to get out there, start killing people, driving fast, and doing drug-peddling missions. Well, it's the same with real life. Okay, not the illegal stuff, but life gets exciting when you step out of your comfort zone and venture into the unknown, you just have to partake is all.

I mean... you know you're going to die, right? Why wouldn't you make the most of now? No one alive today knows what is on the other side. It's comforting to think there is a heaven or an afterlife waiting for us, but none of us know this for a fact. Even hell may not exist. A person could live their life as a murderous, twisted bastard and some of us think they will get what they deserve on their day of judgement. But we don't know that. The truth is, as far as we know, they got to live their life doing whatever the fuck they wanted to do, and ultimately died. Just like the rest of us will. They are no more or no less dead than anyone else could be. So, if you think about it, they basically got away with it all. They had their cake and ate it. And that's what cake is supposed to be there for anyway!

Seriously, putting all beliefs to aside, that is how it is, factually! So, if they get to die and get away with it all, you too can use that same mindset to do whatever you want, hopefully positive and constructive, that will help you live the life you want.

With that being said, you have the permission to make the most of now. It's in this moment you're alive. Not later. Not while thinking about things that happened or will happen. Now! It will take some conditioning to think in the moment all the time, but that is the place where you can be completely free and at peace. Enjoy the moment as much as you can, because one day you will die too. No one else knows if there is anything else on the other side, so live your life now like it is the only one you will get, because as far as we honestly know, it is!

Live truly, live freely, and live completely. Think about it, you'll die either way. You'll die whether you eat yourself into a heart attack, or even if you live your life healthily and die of old age. Death is the only guarantee you have in life. We don't know when our time comes. It could take years by an illness slowly shutting down our bodily functions, or it could be done in the blink of an eye. You will die either way, so as you know this is a 100% fact, why don't you live fully and freely now, and see how far you could really go?

The prospect of death is strong motivation. Death

gives life meaning. Death gives us the urgency to act now because it may be too late otherwise. It gives us energy to live because we know ultimately everything is waning. If we're afraid of death, we end up being afraid of living our lives. We must not be afraid of death. We should always acknowledge our own death. In fact, we should embrace it. Knowing we could die at any time allows us to give more meaning to the current moment. It allows us to take stock of our true reality and experience everything around us fully. By losing your fear of death, you open yourself up to more possibilities, and gain more control over your life.

The next time you feel fear towards a situation, think of your own death. Would you still feel this fear when you are dead? Would this fear hold any control over you when you no longer exist? You could die at any moment. Live your life as if you are about to die in the next second. How attentive to the current moment would you be? Mentally, the closer you are to death, the more alive you feel.

Death is inevitable. As with all fears, becoming familiar with it takes away its strength and ability to control you. Come to terms with death. Understand you will experience death in your lifetime. In the end, you will lose your marriage, you will lose your friendships, you will lose your family, you will lose all the money you made, and all the deals you closed. Every day when the sun dips below the horizon and the sky darkens, you experience the death of another day. Death is a man-made concept. Eventually, it's all going to die. So, it's very simple. Know that everything will die. Be ok with it. Expect it. Accept it. It's the natural progress of every single thing you know to be true. And with that in mind, despite whatever you embark on eventually dying, you can give it your all. You can give your fullest and share yourself with the world. You have nothing to fear. You can live fearlessly and free, because in the end, all our paths lead to the same outcome.

The only variable, the one thing we control to determine the quality of our lives, is the actions we decide to take today.

LEAVE A REVIEW

As an independent self-published author, the reviews section to my book page are extremely important. Reviews really are the lifeblood of any small business and is the only way we can compete with the bigger publishers or sellers on amazon. Without reviews there isn't a chance of any book reaching people. It would simply get buried under all the other books that never get reviewed and never see the light of day.

So, if you liked this book, even just a little bit, or even if your absolutely hated it, I'd really appreciate you leaving an honest review. Either way, it really does help!

Thanks a bunch!

Jay

FURTHER READING

If you enjoyed this book and found it useful check out my website and join my mailing list so I can notify you anytime I upload new content that you also might enjoy. As a subscriber to my website you'll get full access to all articles, eBooks, blog posts, audio content, video content, and you would be first to know when I release other books.

If you'd like specific coaching to improve your abilities with tackling challenges based on the ideas in this book, you can reach me at: jay@jaymistry.net

www.jaymistry.net

Printed in Great Britain
by Amazon

77834583R00099